CW00926883

Usborne Internet help

You can access all the Web sites mentioned in this book quickly and easily by using the Usborne Quicklinks Web site. Just go to **www.usborne-quicklinks.com** and enter the key words **Internet 2002**. This will take you to a page containing direct, regularly updated links to all the sites in the book.

In order to go back to this page whenever you want, you may find it helpful to bookmark it or add it to your "Favorites" list. To do this, click on **Bookmarks** or **Favorites** in your browser's menu bar, then click on **Add**. Once you have done, you can access the page directly from your browser's "Bookmarks" or "Favorites" list.

If you have any problems using the Internet, the guidelines on this page will help you.

Site availability

The links in Usborne Quicklinks are regularly reviewed and updated, but occasionally you may get a message telling you that a site is unavailable. This might be temporary, so try again later, or even the next day.

If any of the recommended sites close down, we will, if possible, replace them with suitable alternatives, so you will always find an up-to-date list of sites in Usborne Quicklinks.

Help

For general help and advice on using the Internet, go to **www.usborne-quicklinks.com** and click on **Net Help**.

To find out more about how to use your Internet browser, click on its **Help** menu and choose **Contents and Index**. You'll find a huge searchable dictionary containing tips on how to find your way around the Internet easily.

For quick and easy access to all the Web sites in this book, go to the Usborne Quicklinks Web site at **www.usborne-quicklinks.com**

Extras

Some Web sites need additional programs, called plug-ins, to play sounds, or to show videos, animations or 3-D images. If you go to a site and you do not have the necessary plug-in, a message saying so will come up on the screen. There is usually a button on the site that you can click on to download the plug-in. Alternatively, go to **www.usborne-quicklinks.com** and click on **Net Help**. There you can find links to download plug-ins.

Here is a list of plug-ins that you might need:
RealPlayer® – lets you play sound and video files.
QuickTime – lets you view video clips.
Flash™ – lets you play animations.
Shockwave® – lets you play animations and interactive programs.

Computer viruses

A computer virus is a program that can seriously damage your computer. A virus can get into your computer when you download programs from the Internet, or from an attachment (an extra file) that arrives with an e-mail.

You can buy anti-virus software at computer stores or download it from the Internet. It is not expensive, and certainly costs less than repairing a damaged computer. At **www.usborne-quicklinks.com** in **Net Help** you'll find a link to the **How Stuff Works** Web site where you can find out more about computer viruses.

Internet safety

All the sites described in this book have been selected by Usborne editors as suitable, in their opinion, for a general audience, although no guarantees can be given and Usborne Publishing is not responsible for the accuracy or suitability of the information on any Web site other than its own.

We recommend that young children are supervised while on the Internet and that children do not use unmonitored Internet chat rooms.

RealPlayer is a trademark of Real Networks, Inc., registered in the US and other countries.
QuickTime is a trademark of Apple Computer, Inc., registered in the US and other countries.
Flash and Shockwave are trademarks of Macromedia, Inc., registered in the US and other countries.

THE USBORNE GUIDE TO
the
internet

2002 EDITION

Mairi Mackinnon

Designed by Russell Punter and Isaac Quaye

Illustrated by Andy Griffin, Russell Punter, Isaac Quaye and Christyan Fox

Managing editor: Jane Chisholm

Technical consultants: Liam Devary, Lisa Hughes and Sally Hughes

With thanks to Ben Denne, Rebecca Gilpin, Asha Kalbag, Mark Wallace, Susanna Davidson and Katarina Dragoslavić

Contents

What's new in the 2002 edition

The Internet is probably the fastest-growing and fastest-changing technology we use in our daily lives. More people are being connected to the Internet all the time, at home, at school or at work. More and more people know what the Internet is, and use it every day to send e-mail and search the World Wide Web.

Thousands of new Web sites are created every day, and existing sites are updated and improved. Sites are closed down, too: in 2000, hundreds of "dotcom" companies were hugely successful for a few months and then disappeared without trace.

Keeping up to date

Because the Internet is changing so fast, it can seem very confusing and hard to keep up. However, the basic technology that makes the Internet work has hardly changed at all in the last eight years: you can find out a little more about it on pages 6-7 of this book.

The main changes are in the hardware and software we use to access the Internet, and the sites we can visit on the World Wide Web. This updated edition of the *Usborne Guide to the Internet* for 2002 reflects those changes, and makes the Internet easier to understand and use.

Easier Internet access

Most people today use a desktop PC and a dial-up modem to access the Internet (find out more about basic hardware on pages 10-11 of this book). However, both modems and computer processors have become much faster over the past few years, making Internet access easier and more reliable, and making it possible for most people to enjoy visiting Web sites with fantastic graphics, animation and high-quality sound. More and more people are able to use high-speed Internet connections such as cable and ADSL, too.

In future, people will be able to access the Internet via their mobile phones, their cars or even their kitchen appliances. You can find out more about Internet devices of this kind on pages 110-113 of this book.

New software

Around 90% of people today use Microsoft® Windows® as their PC operating system, and around 90% use Microsoft® Internet Explorer, which is included in the more recent versions of Windows, as their Internet browser. New for 2002 is Windows®XP, including a new version of Internet Explorer, illustrated in this book. Earlier versions of Internet Explorer included a program called FrontPage® Express, for creating Web sites. FrontPage Express in no longer available, but you can order a trial version of the complete FrontPage program from Microsoft. Pages 80-109 of this book show you how to use FrontPage to design your own Web site.

Changing Web sites

All the Web sites referred to in this book have been checked for 2002, and many new sites have been added. What's more, all the sites can now be accessed easily via Usborne Quicklinks (see below).

Usborne Quicklinks

This book contains references to around 250 Web sites, from in-depth reference sites to games and chat. Sites are being created, updated, moved and closed down all the time. In order to give you the most up-to-date links possible, we have placed links to all the sites on the Usborne Quicklinks Web site at **www.usborne-quicklinks.com**

For more about the Usborne Quicklinks site, and about using the Internet in general, see inside the front cover of this book.

What is the Internet?

The Internet is a vast network of computers linked together, all around the world. It is constantly in the news, and constantly being advertised. Internet services, such as e-mail and the World Wide Web, are an important part of many people's lives, at school, at work or at home.

Over two hundred million people use the Internet worldwide, and millions more are being connected every month. This book will help you to connect to the Internet, and to make the most of your connection.

Why do I need the Internet?

The Internet is a revolutionary way of communicating with people, either one-to-one or with lots of people at once. Whether you want to keep in touch with friends and family anywhere in the world, find information in seconds about any subject under the sun, contact other people who share your interests, or tell people about yourself or your club, organization or company, the Internet makes it easier for you.

What's on the Internet for me?

The most widely-used Internet facilities are:

E-mail This is a way of sending messages via the Internet to another person or group of people. You can easily recognize an e-mail address because it includes the character @ (at). Find out more about it on pages 18-31.

Mailing lists This is a way for people to share information or opinions about a subject via e-mail. Find out more on pages 32-33.

Newsgroups This is another way for people to share their views, but it is more like public notice boards on the Internet that anyone can read. Find out more on pages 34-37.

The World Wide Web This is a huge store of information, including text, pictures, sound and video, which anyone can access from any computer on the Internet. You can recognize an address on the Web because it includes the letters http://www or www. Find out more on pages 38-77.

Chat This is like having a conversation by typing questions and answers. You can "chat" with friends or meet new people, including celebrities. Find out more on pages 78-79.

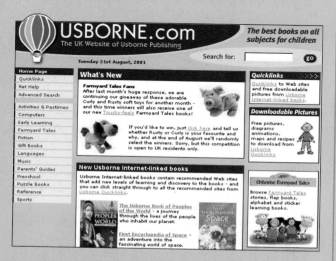

Usborne Publishing uses the Internet to tell people about its books.

Change of address

Web sites are being closed down and new ones are being created all the time. For this reason, the best way to access all the sites referred to in this book is via **www.usborne-quicklinks.com**

The links on Usborne Quicklinks are checked constantly, so if a site has moved, the link to it will be updated, and if a site has closed down, Usborne Quicklinks will try to replace it with a similar one.

Sometimes you may have difficulty accessing a site, even via Usborne Quicklinks. This may be due to a temporary problem with the site's server, so try again a little while later.

Don't panic!

If you are new to the Internet, it can seem huge and confusing, full of complicated technical processes and jargon. This book will help you to get started, explaining what equipment (hardware) and programs (software) you need, and showing you clearly how to connect to the Internet for the first time.

Once you are connected, or "online", it will help you to find your way around, showing you how to use Internet facilities, such as e-mail, mailing lists and newsgroups, and how to search the World Wide Web for information. It will guide you to a range of interesting Web sites, and even show you how to publish information about yourself

by creating your own Web site. Even if you already use the Internet, you will find lots of tips and useful information in this book to save you time and help you to find what you are looking for.

What equipment do I need?

If you are thinking of buying a computer to connect to the Internet, you will find details of exactly what you need on pages 10-11. This book is mainly intended for people using a PC at home, with Microsoft® Windows® 95 or a later version of Windows as the operating system, including Microsoft® Internet Explorer. However, the advice and information in the book will be useful to anyone who wants to use the Internet, no matter what equipment they have.

Is it safe to use the Internet?

Nobody actually owns the Internet, but most of the people and organizations that use it want it to be well-managed and safe. These are some things which might worry people.

Offensive material There is a huge amount of good, interesting and useful information on the Internet. There is also information which is upsetting, untrue and even dangerous. You are very unlikely to find this sort of material if you visit Internet sites run by reputable organizations, of which there are a vast number. There are also ways in which you can block or filter offensive material and prevent it from reaching you or your family. You can find out more about filtering on page 117.

Undesirable people The vast majority of people use the Internet in good faith, but there are a few exceptions. Always think carefully before giving out any personal details, and never arrange to meet up with anyone you have only contacted through the Internet. Find more personal safety advice on page 116.

Viruses Some computer programs, called viruses, can damage your computer, and some of these can be transferred via the Internet. Like viruses in humans, you can take steps to avoid catching them – for example, you can get special programs which make your computer more virus-resistant. Find out more about anti-virus software on pages 116-117.

Shopping on the Internet Many people are concerned about buying and selling goods over the Internet, especially when paying by credit card. It is hard to know who you are dealing with when you only contact someone via a Web site, but most reputable Internet companies take great care of your financial details. You can find out more about safe shopping on page 67.

What's on the Internet?

From messages to music, games to gossip, and academic research to shopping, once you have access to the Internet, you can do a huge variety of things. These pages show you just some of them.

Information

There are millions of computers on the Internet storing millions of files of information which are free for you to view. There are dictionaries, maps, timetables, newspapers and magazines, art galleries, cartoon collections, and information that can help you with your work or hobbies.

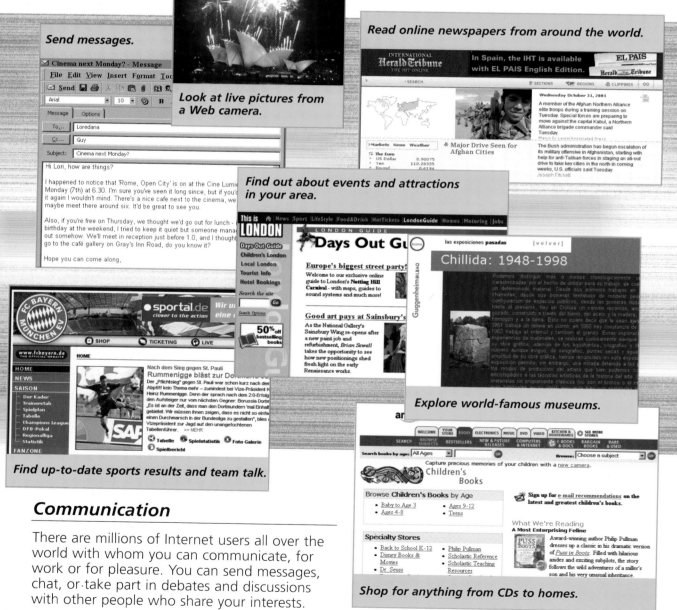

Send messages.

Look at live pictures from a Web camera.

Read online newspapers from around the world.

Find out about events and attractions in your area.

Explore world-famous museums.

Find up-to-date sports results and team talk.

Shop for anything from CDs to homes.

Communication

There are millions of Internet users all over the world with whom you can communicate, for work or for pleasure. You can send messages, chat, or take part in debates and discussions with other people who share your interests.

Find out about destinations around the world.

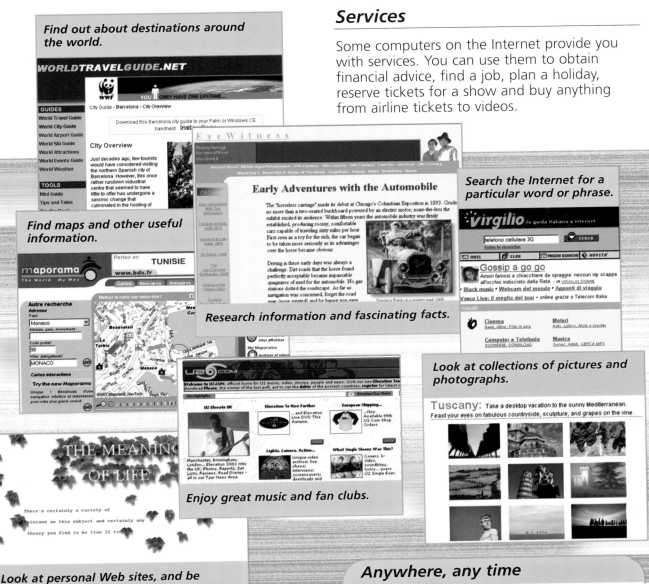

Services

Some computers on the Internet provide you with services. You can use them to obtain financial advice, find a job, plan a holiday, reserve tickets for a show and buy anything from airline tickets to videos.

Find maps and other useful information.

Search the Internet for a particular word or phrase.

Research information and fascinating facts.

Look at collections of pictures and photographs.

Enjoy great music and fan clubs.

Look at personal Web sites, and be inspired to create your own.

Programs

There are lots of programs available for you to copy onto your computer. Some are free to use; others you'll need to pay for. You can find programs for listening to music, watching video clips or playing games, as well as the latest programs to help you use the Internet more efficiently.

Anywhere, any time

You can connect to the Internet 24 hours a day, seven days a week, anywhere in the world. You can use a computer at home, at school or at work, or a public computer in a library or café. You can even use a portable device, such as a PDA (Personal Digital Assistant, see page 11) or a mobile phone. The Internet can be a part of your everyday life, wherever you are in the world.

How does the Internet work?

The Internet is a vast network linking together millions of computers all over the world.

What is a network?

A network is a group of computers and computer equipment which have been linked together so that they can share information and resources. The computers in an office, for example, are often networked so that they can open the same files and use the same printers.

All the computers linked to the Internet can exchange information with each other. It's as easy to communicate with a computer on the other side of the world as with one that is right next door.

Once your own computer is connected to the Internet, it is like a spider in the middle of a huge web. All the threads of the web can bring you information from other computers. If one computer in the network isn't working, your computer can still fetch the information using different threads.

Servers and clients

There are two main types of computers on the Internet. The ones which store, sort and distribute information are called servers. They are powerful computers that are always switched on, so that the information is always available. Those that access this information, such as your computer at home, are called clients. A server computer serves a client computer, like a store owner helping a customer.

The picture below shows how the computers in different organizations in a town are linked together by the Internet.

People can connect their computers at home to the Internet.

Cables and telephone lines link one part of the network to another.

At school, children can use the Internet to learn and to communicate with children in other countries.

Universities all over the world can use the Internet to share their research information.

People can use the computers at this café to connect to the Internet and send and receive messages.

Communication lines

The network of computers that makes up the Internet is linked together by private and public telephone systems. Computer information is translated into telephone signals and sent from one computer to another in seconds. The cables that link computer networks range from ordinary telephone cables, made of copper, to fibre optic cables, made of thin glass strands. Fibre optic cables can carry huge amounts of information, up to a thousand times faster than copper cable. They are often used for "backbone" connections, which are the most important links between the largest computers on the Internet.

Networks can also be linked by satellite, microwaves, radio waves and infra-red. Networks in different countries and continents are linked by satellite and by large undersea fibre optic cables.

This computer belongs to a company that provides people at home or in offices with access to the Internet.

Businesses can use the Internet to exchange information and to sell their products.

Computer talk

To make sure that all the computers on the Internet can communicate with each other, they all use the same language. It is called TCP/IP (Transmission Control Protocol/ Internet Protocol), and it ensures that when data is sent from one computer to another, it is always transmitted in a particular way and it arrives safely in the right place.

Every computer on the Internet has a unique address, which is actually a long number called an IP (Internet Protocol) number. This enables computers to find each other across the Internet. When you type any Internet address into your computer, your computer converts it into an IP number address in order to send information to the right place.

When one computer sends a piece of information to another computer, the information is broken down into small "packets" of data. Each packet carries the IP number address, specifying where the information has come from and where it is going. The packets travel via the Internet to the destination computer where they are reassembled.

The data that forms this picture is broken into packets.

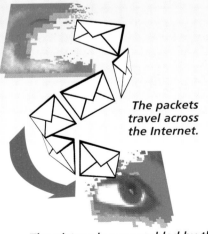

The packets travel across the Internet.

The picture is reassembled by the destination computer.

What hardware do I need?

Today, many computers are sold as "Internet ready", which means that they have all the hardware and software you need to go online.

However, you don't need a brand new computer to use the Internet. If you have a PC which has at least a 486 processor chip, you will be able to connect to the Internet. If you are using a Macintosh computer, it will need a 68030 processor or better.

Your computer

To use the Internet, your computer will need at least 32 megabytes (MB) of RAM. RAM (Random Access Memory) is the part of your computer's memory which enables it to use programs. Memory is measured in bytes, and 1 megabyte (MB) is just over a million bytes.

Software, and any other information you want to save permanently, is stored on your computer's hard disk. Your computer needs at least 100MB of free hard disk space to store Internet software. (Free space is storage space that isn't being used by other programs.)

Internet connection software (see pages 12-13) is usually supplied on CD, so you will find it easier to get started on the Internet if you have a CD or DVD drive on your computer.

Pictures and sound

You may want to use the Internet to watch video clips, listen to music or play games. All Macintosh computers, and all multimedia PCs (PCs designed to play CDs or DVDs) with Pentium processors, can play video and sound files. If you have an older or more basic model, you may need to install some extra hardware.

Video To enjoy the animation and videos that are available on the Internet, your computer needs a powerful graphics card. If your computer doesn't have the right kind of card, the pictures will be fuzzy and will move slowly. You need at least a 32 bit card with 2MB of Video RAM (VRAM).

Sound If you want to hear sounds on the Internet, such as music and video clips or voice recordings, your computer will need to have a sound card and speakers.

If you are installing graphics or sound cards, it's best to have them fitted by an expert.

Sound cards

This is a multimedia PC. It has an internal modem.

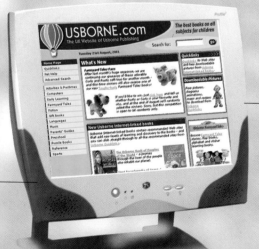

Monitor, or screen, and CPU (Central Processing Unit). The computer's hard drive is stored inside here.

Speaker

Keyboard

Mouse

Modems

The easiest way to connect to the Internet is by using a device called a modem. This connects your computer to a telephone line and translates computer information into telephone signals and back again. There are three kinds of modems: hardware internal and external modems and software modems. Internal modems fit inside your computer's processing unit, and many new computers have them already installed. An external modem sits on your desk, and has a cable which plugs into one of the sockets in your computer's processing unit. This socket is called a serial port. Hand-held devices, such as PDAs and mobile phones, use software modems in order to make them light and portable.

An external modem

Modem speed

Modems send and receive information at different speeds. The speed is measured in bits per second (bps). It is best to have the fastest modem you can afford, at least 33,600 bps (33.6Kbps or 33K) and ideally 56,600 bps (56K). If you have a high-speed modem, you will spend less time waiting for pictures or information to appear on the screen. Waiting for information is frustrating, and can be expensive if you are paying for the time you are online.

Your telephone line

You must be able to plug your modem into a telephone point near your computer. If you have only one telephone line, you won't be able to make or receive telephone calls while you are connected to the Internet.

Connecting without a PC

PDAs and mobile phones These devices can send and receive e-mail or shorter text messages. Some can also connect to the World Wide Web, or to special information pages that have been adapted so that they are easier to read on a small screen. You can find out more about them on pages 112-113.

Set-top boxes and consoles Using a device called a set-top box, you can browse the World Wide Web and collect e-mail via your television. Some games consoles can also connect to the Internet. However, it is hard to send e-mail or other information yourself without a keyboard and full-power computer.

Super-fast connections

For most people connecting to the Internet from home, an ordinary modem is fast enough for their needs. However, speedier connections are available and becoming more popular, although generally they cost more to install and use.

ISDN connection An ISDN line can send and receive data much more efficiently than a modem. It is also much faster, at up to 128Kbps.

Satellite connection You can receive Internet information via satellite at very high speeds, but to send data yourself you will still need an ordinary telephone modem.

DSL or **ADSL** New technology makes it possible to use your existing telephone line to send and receive data up to ten times faster than a 56K modem.

Internet Service Providers

To connect your computer to the Internet, you will need to sign up with an Internet Service Provider or ISP (sometimes called an Internet Access Provider).

What is an ISP?

An ISP is a company that specializes in connecting people to the Internet. It has a network of server computers across the country or even around the world. You connect to the ISP through your modem and the telephone network, and the ISP gives you access to the Internet.

An ISP will provide you with the software you need to go online. It will set up an e-mail address for you, and send and receive your e-mail. It will also have a telephone helpline, or technical support service, which you can call if you have any difficulties in connecting.

For these services some ISPs charge a small monthly fee.

These are some popular ISPs from around the world.

How do I choose an ISP?

There are hundreds of ISPs to choose from. Before you decide on one, talk to friends who are already online. Ask them if they would recommend the ISP they use.

Internet magazines regularly review and rank ISPs, so look out for current issues with ISP reviews. If you can access the Internet on another computer, you'll find links to some reviews on the Usborne Quicklinks site at **www.usborne-quicklinks.com** You'll also find details of some ISPs on page 123.

Finally, talk to an ISP before you make a decision. In the box below, there are some important questions you should ask them.

Questions to ask an ISP

 Do you have a start-up charge? Try to avoid paying a charge just to sign up with an ISP, as you will lose the money if you decide to move to another one.

 Is there a monthly fee? Some ISPs charge a small amount every month for their services. See whether this pays for a certain amount of time online free of charge, for example using a freecall number to connect to the Internet.

 Do you have different price plans? Sometimes you can choose to pay a little more each month in order to have more free hours online. Think about how much you expect to use the Internet, and choose a price plan that suits you. Make sure you can change from one price plan to another if you find your Internet use is changing.

 Can I connect to the Internet for the cost of a local call? Most large ISPs use either a local call rate number or a freecall number to connect you to the Internet. You certainly shouldn't have to pay more than the cost of a local call for the time you spend online.

 When can I call your helpline, and how much does it cost? Some ISPs have technical support lines open 24 hours a day, free of charge. With others, you can pay a small monthly or annual charge, and then call the helpline free of charge as often as you need.

You may have to pay to call other helplines, and they may not be open all day or every day, especially if the ISP is intended mainly for business users. Make sure the helpline will be available when you need it.

Connection software

An ISP will provide you with all the software you need to get connected to the Internet. Many ISPs give away free CDs with this software; you'll find these CDs in lots of shops and in computer magazines. Other companies will send you the software if you call and ask them for it.

Free services

A number of ISPs offer free Internet access. This means that you do not pay the ISP a monthly charge (although you may still have to pay your telephone company for the time you spend online).

These ISPs may charge higher rates for calls to their helplines: a ten-minute call to discuss a problem can be expensive. If you have not used the Internet before, you may prefer to start with an ISP which has a free helpline. After all, you can always change your ISP when you are more experienced.

Other ISPs offer unmetered access – unlimited Internet access for a small monthly charge. You connect to the Internet using a freecall number, so you don't have to pay anything to your telephone company. This is worth while if you use the Internet for more than a few hours a week, so see if your ISP offers unmetered access as an option – you might choose to take it up in the future.

Do you offer support for Macs?
If you have a Macintosh computer, make sure the ISP's helpline offers suitable technical support.

Is your service suitable for my modem type?
Tell the ISP what kind of modem you have, and your modem speed. You may need to tell them the "modem standard" – you can check this in your modem manual.

What software do you supply?
If you are using Microsoft® Windows® 95 or a later version of Windows, your ISP should be able to supply its own Internet connection software on CD, ready for you to install. They may also include useful extras, such as a Web browser (see page 38) and e-mail program, if you don't have them already.

If you are using any other operating system, make sure the ISP can provide you with the right software.

How many e-mail addresses can I have? And how much Web space?
You may not need unlimited e-mail addresses (although some ISPs offer them), but if you are connecting to the Internet at home, it is useful to have different addresses for different members of the family.

Many ISPs also offer space you can use for your own Web site (find out how to build a Web site on pages 80-109 of this book).

Online services

Some ISPs, called online services, not only connect you to the Internet, but also offer you a whole selection of news, information and communication services of their own.

Why choose an online service?

Online services are a very popular way of connecting to the Internet as they are easy to use and have many useful features for their members. They have lots of information which is available to their members only. You can keep up with the news and find out about films, music, sport, money matters, travel and hobbies.

You can also "chat" with other members who share your interests. This is like having a conversation, using your keyboard to type questions and answers. As you type, your messages appear on the other members' screens, and they can type their responses.

Sometimes famous people are invited to join organized chat sessions, and you can ask them questions online. If you have friends who use online services, "messenger services" tell you when they are online at the same time as you so that you can chat with them. You can find out more about chat sessions and messenger services on pages 78-79.

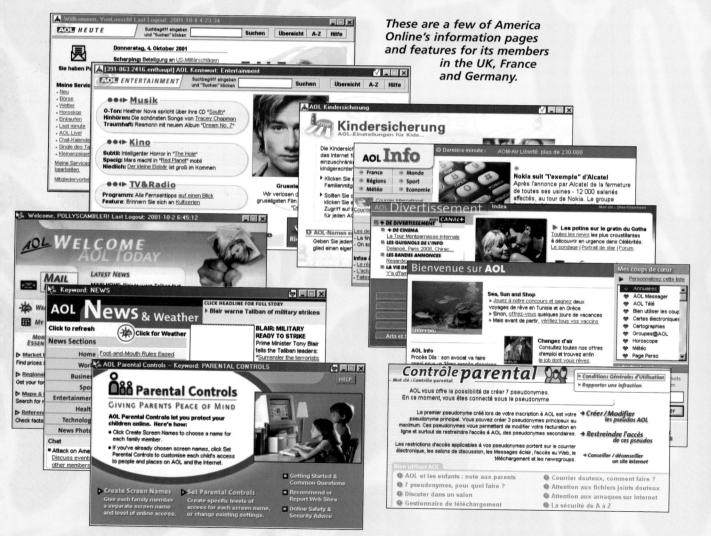

These are a few of America Online's information pages and features for its members in the UK, France and Germany.

Which one is best for me?

The best-known online services are America Online (AOL) and CompuServe. You can call their sales departments for free connection software CDs, and they generally offer a free trial period. After that you will pay a small monthly charge for using the service. You can find telephone numbers for AOL and CompuServe on page 123 of this book.

Different online services suit different people. America Online has a useful feature called "parental controls", for parents who want to protect their children from unpleasant or upsetting material on the Internet. Parental controls can be set so that AOL blocks Internet sites with upsetting content, meaning that children should not find them even by accident. AOL can also act as a good guide to the World Wide Web, helping you to find your way around and directing you to interesting sites.

CompuServe is popular with business users, as it offers plenty of up-to-date financial information and good links to business services.

CompuServe has useful information for businesses and professional people.

The Microsoft® Network

The Microsoft Network (MSN®) is similar to an online service, but it is available to everybody who has access to the World Wide Web. You can call for a free connection software CD and use MSN as your ISP (you'll find the telephone number on page 123), or you can use a different ISP and connect to MSN via the Web.

MSN has home pages for different countries all around the world.

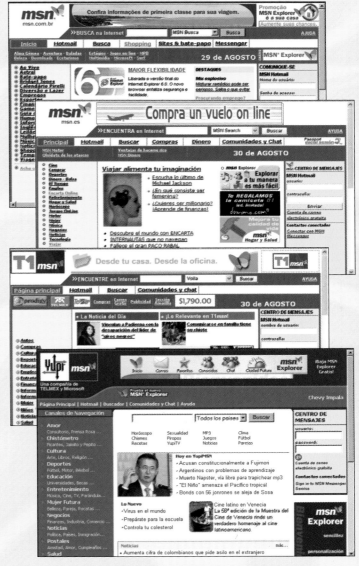

Connecting for the first time

Once you have decided on an ISP or an online service, and received a CD from them, you are ready to install your Internet connection software.

Installing the software

First of all, make sure your computer modem is connected and switched on. Close any programs running on your computer and insert the CD in your computer's CD drive. The installation should start automatically, and instructions will appear on the screen.

You may be asked to restart your computer in order to complete the installation process. You may also be asked to key in a registration number and password; you will find these on the CD cover. If you have any difficulties, you can call the customer support number which you should find on the CD cover.

Choosing a user name

You will then be asked to choose a "username" or "screen name", and your own password. Your username will be used as part of your e-mail address, and you can choose any name you like, as long as nobody else has chosen it already. Everyone who uses the same ISP or online service has a different username, so try to think of a few possible names in case your first choice has been taken by someone else.

You can generally use full stops, hyphens (–) or underscores (_) as part of a username; you can't use commas, spaces, slashes (/) or brackets. Sometimes you can combine names and numbers; if your name is Anne Jackson, and someone has already chosen anne.jackson, you could be anne.jackson1 or anne.jackson24 (the number could be your birthday).

> Max.S?
> Max.Surfer?
> Max.Surfer_1?

Password tips

Lots of services on the Internet ask you to enter a password, so try to think of one word which you can use every time. Passwords usually have to be between four and ten letters long. If you think you might forget your password, make a note of it somewhere safe.

Choose a password that you will remember but anyone else will find difficult to guess. Never tell anyone else your password – you should only ever have to enter it on screen.

When you have finished

Once you have finished installing the software, a message should appear on screen to tell you that the installation was successful.

When you restart your computer, you will see your ISP's icon on your desktop. Double-clicking on this icon will connect you to your ISP, and through your ISP to the Internet.

⚠ Virus warning

A virus is a program that damages a computer by destroying information stored on its hard disk. It is possible to pick up a virus over the Internet, especially via e-mail. Before you set up an Internet connection, make sure you have anti-virus software installed on your computer. This will work while you are online, and should identify and stop viruses before they can do any damage.

Many new computers have anti-virus software already installed, but check that you have the most up-to-date version and make sure it is updated every few months. New viruses are being invented all the time by people who want to cause damage on the Internet, and software manufacturers are constantly finding ways of fighting new types.

You can find out where to look for anti-virus software on the Internet on page 117.

Making a connection

When you connect to your ISP for the first time, a Dial-up Connection window will appear like the one below, and you will be asked to type in your password. The first two boxes in the window should have your ISP's name and your user name already filled in. If you fill in your password and then click on the *Save password* box, you will not have to type the password again every time you go online.

Click on the *Connect* button. Your modem will dial the number to connect to your ISP. Below the *Connect* button you may see details of how your connection is progressing. When your modem has made a connection, this window will disappear.

Going online

Once you have a connection, you will be able to open a program called a browser, or it may open automatically. You can find out more about browsers and how to use them on pages 38-43. Inside the browser window will appear your ISP's "home page". This looks a little like the front page of a newspaper.

If you have chosen an online service, the first thing you see when you go online will be a "welcome page". This may have snippets of the day's news, or other information which you might find interesting.

This is the Dial-up Connection window.

Type your password in this space.

Click on this button to connect.

This window shows you what is happening as your modem dials your ISP.

This is the browser window.

This is an ISP's home page.

About e-mail

E-mail, or electronic mail, is one of the most popular facilities on the Internet. You can send a message from your computer to another computer half way around the world, and it could arrive in less than a minute.

E-mail users find ordinary mail so slow that they call it "snail mail". E-mail is also much cheaper than normal mail: you can send a message anywhere in the world for the cost of a short local phone call.

How does it work?

Sending e-mail is like sending any other kind of information via the Internet. When you send your message, it is broken down into packets (see page 9) and sent from one computer to another until it reaches its destination.

Do I need special software?

If you have a browser installed on your computer, or if your ISP has provided you with one, you should find that it includes an e-mail program. Netscape®'s e-mail program is called Netscape® Messenger. The examples in this book use a program called Microsoft® Outlook® Express, which is part of Microsoft® Internet Explorer. Don't worry if you have a different program – most e-mail programs work in a similar way.

Online services also include e-mail programs: AOL incorporates AOL Mail. You can also buy e-mail software; for example, Microsoft® Outlook® is a more advanced version of Outlook Express.

Web-based e-mail

You can use e-mail even if you don't have a direct Internet connection of your own. There are several e-mail services on the World Wide Web, such as Hotmail®, which allow you to send and receive e-mail from any computer anywhere in the world. Find out more about these services on pages 76-77.

E-mail addresses

To send an e-mail, you need to have an e-mail address yourself and you need to know the e-mail address of the person you are sending it to. When you sign up with an ISP, you will be given your own, unique e-mail address, based on your username (see page 16). All e-mail addresses are made up of the same three elements: a username, an @ symbol ("at"), and a domain name. Here is a typical address:

mairi@usborne.co.uk
User name   "At"   Domain name

A user name is usually the person's name or nickname. A domain name might be their ISP's name or the name of the company where they work. The domain name is followed by a few letters which tell you something about the domain – maybe what sort of organization it is, and maybe where it is based.

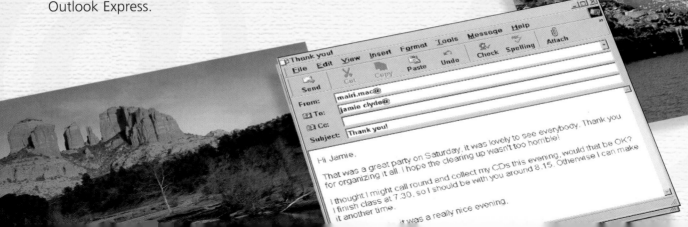

What do the letters mean?

.co or **.com**	a commercial organization
.ac or **.edu**	an educational establishment
.gov	a government organization
.org	an organization, usually not commercial (such as a charity)
.net	an Internet company

From 2003, there will also be several new codes including **.biz** for businesses.

There are hundreds of different country codes. Here are just a few of them:

.uk	based in the UK
.ie	based in Ireland
.ca	based in Canada
.au	based in Australia

Domain names in the US don't have a country code, they just end in **.com**, **.edu**, **.org** etc.

As well as text messages, you can send e-cards to your friends, like the ones shown here.

An e-mail message tells a friend that you have sent them an e-card, and connects them to a Web site where they can see the e-card and a message from you.

How do I find someone's address?

The easiest way to find out someone's e-mail address is to ask them. It's best to write the address down, and make sure you have it exactly right – even one missing dot or hyphen will mean your message can't be delivered.

You could also give the person your own e-mail address and ask them to send you an e-mail; their address will appear at the top of their message.

Always keep a record of e-mail addresses, as they can be very difficult to remember exactly. E-mail programs include an address book where you can store addresses – find out more about this on page 27.

This is an animated e-card.

19

Sending e-mail

This is the opening window of Outlook Express.

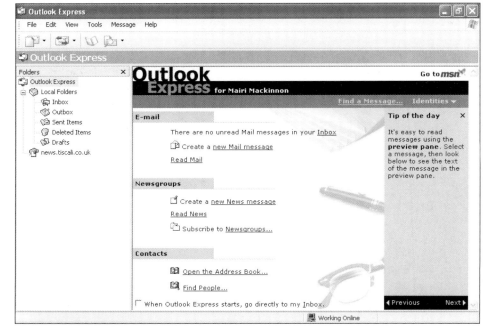

On these pages you will find out how to send an e-mail using Microsoft® Outlook® Express. Even if you have a different e-mail program, you will still find that the steps are very similar.

Getting started

To open your e-mail program, look for the program's icon on your computer desktop and double-click on it. You can also open the program by selecting it in your *Programs* menu (to open this, click on the *Start* button at the bottom left-hand corner of the screen, and then click on *Programs*).

If you are using AOL or CompuServe, go to the Mail Room or Mail Centre. You will find links to these on the Welcome page.

Making a connection

If you connect to the Internet via an ISP, the Dial-up Connection window will appear on top of your e-mail program window – see page 17 to remind yourself what to do next.

If you have already chosen the option *Save password*, all you have to do is click on the *Connect* button, and your modem will dial your ISP and try to connect you. You may hear strange squealing sounds while this is happening. This is your modem working; the sounds will stop once the connection has been made.

Working offline

If you are sending a long message, or several messages, disconnect from the Internet and write your messages "offline". Otherwise you will have to pay your telephone company for all the time you spend working on your messages before you send them. Even if you do not have to pay for your time online, while your modem is plugged into your telephone line, nobody will be able to call you.

To disconnect from the Internet, look for the the command *Sign Off* (for AOL members), *Access - Disconnect* (for CompuServe) or *Work Offline*. In Outlook Express, *Work Offline* is in the *File* menu.

Sending a message

To make sure that your e-mail is working, try sending a message to yourself.

(1) Click on "Create a <u>new Mail message</u>" or click on the *Write Message* (or *New Mail*) button at the top left-hand corner of the Outlook Express window.

(2) A New Message window will appear.

(3) Click in the *To* box and type in your own e-mail address.

(4) Click in the *Subject* box and type **Test**. This is called the message's "subject line".

(5) Click in the main message area, and type **Test message**.

(6) Click on the *Send* button at the top left-hand corner of the window. If you are working online, the New Message window will close, and you will be able to see the main Outlook Express window again. You may see a **(1)** appear next to the Outbox for a moment. You may also see the message "Sending mail..." at the bottom right-hand corner of the Outlook Express window.

(7) If you are working offline, a window will appear telling you that your message will be stored in the Outbox until you are ready to send it. Click *OK*.

(8) When you are ready to go online, click on the *Send/Recv* button at the top of the window. A window will ask you whether you want to go online. When you click *Yes*, the Dial-Up Connection window will appear.

(9) Another window will appear to tell you that your e-mail program is sending your message. The window will close when your message has been sent.

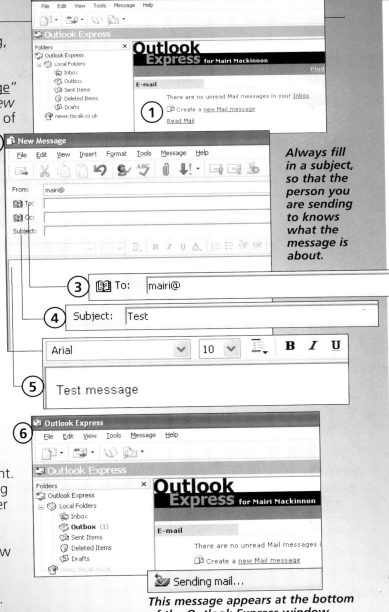

Always fill in a subject, so that the person you are sending to knows what the message is about.

This message appears at the bottom of the Outlook Express window.

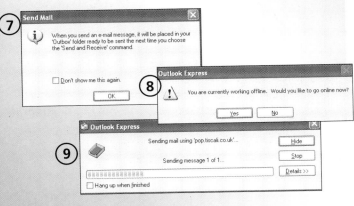

Receiving e-mail

When someone sends you an e-mail, your ISP server stores it in a place called your mailbox.

You need to go online to collect e-mail from your mailbox and transfer it to your computer. This is known as downloading your messages.

Reading a new message

If you sent yourself a test message by following the instructions on page 21, you can collect it now.

① Open up Outlook® Express. Once your modem has connected, you may see the message "Receiving mail..." at the bottom right-hand corner of the Outlook Express window.

② You will see a **(1)** next to the Inbox in your Folders list, and the message "There is 1 unread Mail message in your Inbox".

③ Click on Inbox in the Folders list, or click on this message, and your Inbox window will open. It has two halves. In the top half you will see your message with a closed envelope icon (unread message) which changes to an open envelope icon (read message). In the bottom half you will see the beginning of your message.

④ If you double-click on the envelope icon or anywhere on the line beside it showing your name and the Subject line, a message window will open, showing you the message in full. The header (the area above the message window) gives you details of the message – who sent it, its subject and when it was sent.

⑤ If you want to print out a copy of a message, check that your printer is switched on and ready, then click on the *Print* button in the Toolbar at the top of the screen.

⑥ If you don't want to keep the message once you have read it, click on the *Delete* button in the Toolbar.

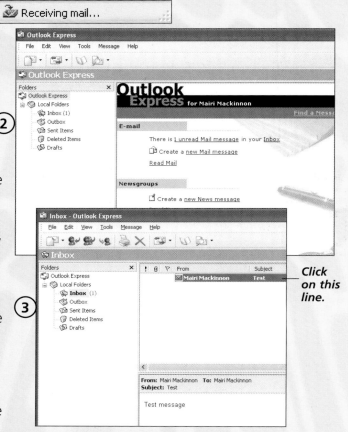

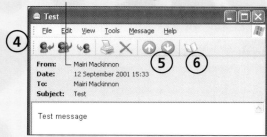

Click on this line.

This part is the message header.

Replying and forwarding

It's easy to respond to an e-mail. You can send a reply, or send a message on to someone else with your own comments added.

When you receive a message, you will see two or three buttons above or beside the message. Clicking on one of these buttons will open a new message window containing the original message and space for your reply or your comments.

Replying to a message

 When you click on the *Reply* button, a new message window appears, addressed to the person who sent the original message. The subject line begins "Re:", followed by the original subject.

The Reply window looks like this.

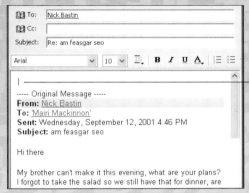

Type your answer in this area.

When you start typing, your text appears at the top of the main message window. The original message appears below. You can delete this part if you want, to make your message shorter and easier to read.

Replying to all

If you receive a message that has been sent to a group of people (see "Sending to more than one person", right) you can send a reply to everyone in that group. When you click on the *Reply All* button, a new message window will appear like the Reply window above, but it will be addressed to everybody in the group.

Forwarding a message

 To send a message on to another person, click on the *Forward* button. A new message window will appear, like the Reply window, but you will need to fill in the address of the person you are sending the message on to. The subject line begins "Fw:", followed by the original subject.

The Forward window looks like this.

Fill in the person's e-mail address.

You can type your own comments in this area.

If you want to add anything to the message, start typing and your comments will appear at the top of the main message window, with the original message below.

Sending to more than one person

You can send or forward an e-mail to several different people at the same time. Just type their addresses in the *To* box, separated by ; (a semicolon), like this:

dad@home.net; alex@work.com; kate@work.org

You can also send a copy of the e-mail to one or more people, to let them know what you have said. Type their addresses in the *Cc* box, separated by a semicolon if you are sending copies to more than one address.

Writing good messages

"Hello", no, er.."Hi"... "Hiya"..?

When you first send e-mail, you may feel awkward and your messages may be rather stiff and formal. When you are used to sending e-mail, on the other hand, it's easy to be careless and even say things you don't really mean. This section will help you to write messages which are clear and easy to read.

Tips for good messages

@ Always give your message a subject, saying briefly and clearly what the message is about. For example, "Any plans for Saturday night?" is much clearer than just "Saturday", and easier to read than "I wondered if you were doing anything on Saturday night."

@ Keep your messages fairly short and simple. It can be tiring to read a long message on a computer screen.

@ If your message is fairly long, use short paragraphs and spaces in between paragraphs, to make it easier to read.

@ When you are replying to a message, or forwarding one, don't include all of the original message. Delete the parts which aren't important (find out how to do this on the next page).

@ Don't use bold or italic letters, as different e-mail programs from yours may not show them when they display a message. You can emphasize a word or phrase by putting *asterisks around it*, like this.

@ Check your spelling. It's easy to write a message in a hurry and then send it before you notice silly mistakes. Read through the message carefully on the screen before you send it; you might like to use the spelling checker if your e-mail program has one. In Microsoft® Outlook® Express, the spelling checker is in the *Options* menu (see page 26).

Hope you are feling betta.

@ Don't send messages in capital letters. This is the e-mail equivalent of SHOUTING!

@ Don't reply to a message in too much of a hurry. When you answer a letter, you have a little more time to think about your answer before you post it, but it's easy to send a hasty reply to an e-mail and then regret it. Sending angry or rude e-mail is called "flaming".

@ Be careful if you are including funny comments. When you are speaking to somebody face to face or on the telephone, it is easy for them to tell if you are joking, but people can mistake the tone of an e-mail. If you think you might be misunderstood, you can always add a "smiley" (see page 33).

@ Be careful what you write. E-mail is not always private, and messages can accidentally be sent to the wrong person.

@ It's polite to reply to e-mails as soon as you can. With a letter, you could leave your reply for a few days, but with e-mail people may expect a reply within a day. If you know you can't answer right away, you can always send a brief message to let the other person know you have received their message and will answer properly as soon as you are able to.

Editing a message

When you are replying to a message, or forwarding one (see page 23), the original message will appear in the new message window. Normally your answer will appear above the original message.

You can delete part or all of the original message. You should definitely do this when you are replying to a reply (or even a reply to a reply), otherwise every message in the sequence appears every time, and the messages become impossibly long.

Select the part you want to delete. Highlight it by clicking at the beginning and dragging your mouse cursor to the end of the text you want to delete. Then press the *Delete* key on your keyboard.

You can also quote sections of text by highlighting them in this way and using the *Edit* – *Copy* and *Paste* commands in the menu bar.

Your answer will appear here, at the top.

Earlier messages may appear inside arrow signs, like this.

You may want to delete this, your original message.

After editing, your reply might look like this.

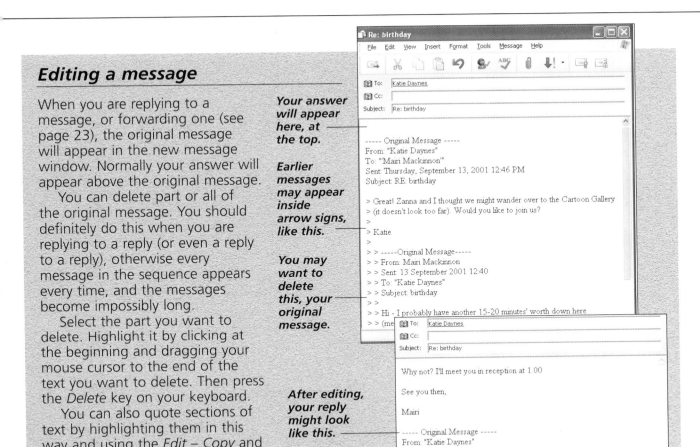

Replying to specific points

You can choose to answer the points made in a message one by one. To do this, edit the message as much as you need to, as described above. Then place your cursor after the point you are replying to, press the Return key and type your answer. Leave one line space before and after your replies.

Some e-mail programs use arrows before each line in the original message. The person you are replying to can see which lines are your replies, as they don't have any arrows. Some e-mail programs use indents – starting the line a little further to the right – instead of arrows. Others show the text of replies in a different colour, although the colour may not come out in a different e-mail program, so it's best always to leave space before and after your replies to make them clear.

This is part of the original message.

This is part of the reply.

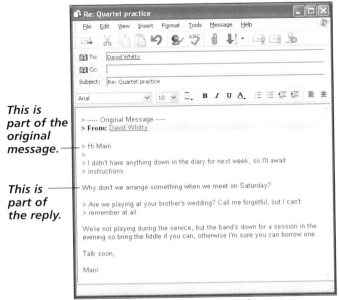

This reply answers points one by one.

Personalizing your e-mail program

Once you know how to send and receive messages, there are several ways in which you can personalize your e-mail program. You can change the look of your messages and add a personal signature. You can also create an address book for e-mail addresses you use often.

A shortcut to your Inbox

You can set up Microsoft® Outlook® Express so that when you open the program, you see your Inbox and any new messages in it right away.

When you open Outlook Express, you will see an option at the bottom of the screen: "When Outlook Express starts, go directly to my Inbox". Click on the box beside this option.

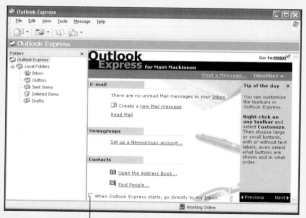

Click here to open your Inbox directly.

Outlook Express options

Most of the commands for personalizing Outlook Express are in the Options window. To open this window, click on *Tools* on the menu bar, and then *Options...* A window will appear like the one below.

Click on any of the headings across the top of the window to bring up a different set of options. You can change the settings for sending and receiving mail, checking spelling before you send a message or adding your own signature (see below).

Choose options from these headings.

Click here to add the signature to all your messages.

Type your signature text here.

Click OK.

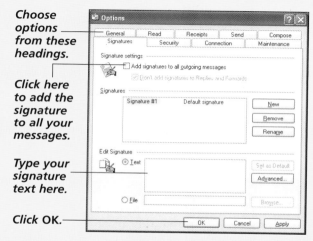

This is the Options window for creating a personal signature.

E-mail signatures

An e-mail signature could include your name, nickname or slogan, a joke or a quotation. If you use e-mail at work, you might want to give your department name or your job title. Otherwise it's best not to include personal information such as your home address.

E-mail signatures can also include pictures made up of keystrokes. If you try this, keep the picture fairly simple as it may not look quite the same in a different e-mail program.

These are examples of e-mail signatures.

The picture on the right is made up of keystrokes.

```
              \\ | | | | / / / 7
              \\ | | | | / | | //
              /   ~ | ~ |      nnn
             --\   0 | 0 /   n| | | |
             \ ?   _ \ \    | | \
             U\   \_/ \    \_/
               \_____/     &&&
             &&&/__ /&&&&  &&&
             &&&&&&&&&&&&&&&&
             &&&&&&&&&&&&&&&
             &&&&&&&&&&&&&&
*****************************************
"Nìl sa saol seo ach ceo is nì bheimìd beo
ach seal beag gearr."
("It's a misty old world, and we are only in
it for a short, sharp while") - Irish proverb.
*****************************************
```

Creating an address book

You don't need to type in someone's e-mail address every time you send them an e-mail. You can save addresses in an address book, and select one when you start a new message.

(1) Click on the *Addresses* button in the Toolbar.

(2) An Address Book window will open. Click on the *New* button and select *New Contact...*

(3) A Properties window will open. You can enter as many details as you like about the person by clicking on the keywords across the top of the window, but you should at least enter their name and e-mail address.

(4) When you have entered the details, click *OK*. The Properties window will close and you will see your new contact listed in your address book.

(5) Close the Address Book. If you want to send an e-mail to someone in the book, click on the *New Mail* button in the Toolbar. A New Message window will open.

(6) Click on the Address Book symbol next to the *To* button. A Select Recipients window will appear with a list of your contacts. Click on the name of the person you are writing to, and then click on the *To* button to the right of the list. Your contact's name will appear in the box beside the *To* button.

(7) Click *OK*. The Select Recipients window will close, and your contact's name will appear in the *To* box of your message header.

You can choose to have e-mail addresses added to your address book automatically when you reply to an e-mail. To do this, click on *Tools* in the menu bar, then select *Options...* and then *Send*. You will see the option *Automatically put people I reply to in my Address Book*. Make sure there is a tick in the box beside this option.

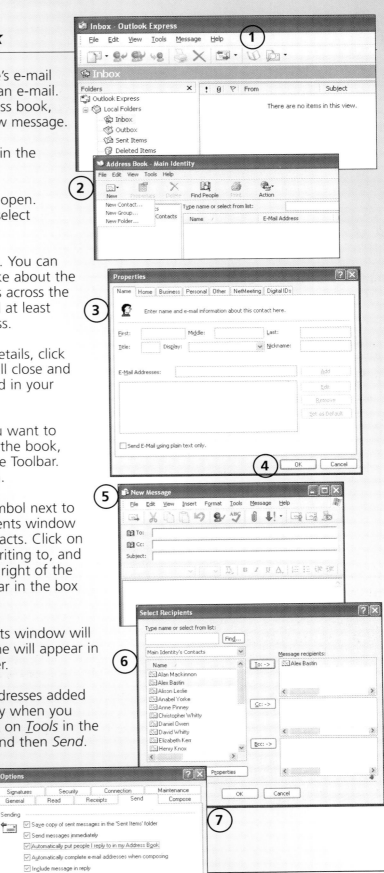

Organizing your e-mail

When you start sending and receiving lots of messages, you will find your Inbox and your Sent Items folders soon fill up with old messages. You may want to keep some of these; others you may want to delete permanently. These pages show you how to organize your messages, making your e-mail program much easier to use.

Deleting messages

To delete a message in any of your folders, click on it to select it. Then click on the *Delete* button at the top of the screen.

Your message will be sent to the Deleted Items folder, but it will not be deleted permanently. If you decide that you still need it after all, click on the Deleted Items folder. Click on the message and hold your mouse button down as you drag your message back into the Inbox. Your mouse cursor will change to a ⊘ symbol, which becomes an arrow again once it is over your Inbox. Release the button, and the message will be left in your Inbox.

You can also move a message by selecting it, clicking on *Edit* in the menu at the top of the screen, and then clicking on *Move to Folder...* This will open a "Move" window, and you can choose the folder where you want to store the message.

Deleting messages permanently

From time to time, you will need to empty your Deleted Items folder. To do this, click on the folder and select all the messages by clicking on the first message, holding down the Shift key and clicking on the last message in the list. Then click on the *Delete* button. A message will appear asking whether you are sure you want to delete the messages. Click on *Yes* and the messages will be deleted.

Click on Yes to delete messages.

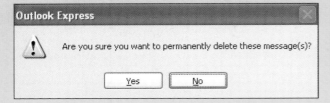

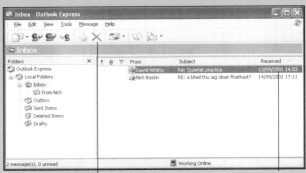

Delete *button*   *This message is selected.*

⚠ Is this for me?

If you receive an e-mail from an address you don't recognize, the safest thing is to delete it without opening it.

Some e-mail, called "spam", is like the junk mail sent through the postal system. When you give your e-mail address, for example when you are filling in a form on a Web site, look for a box you can tick if you don't want to receive advertising e-mail.

If you repeatedly get messages you don't want from the same source, try filtering or blocking them. In Outlook Express, do this by clicking on *Message* in the Menu bar, then on *Block Sender*. All future messages from that address will be sent straight to your Deleted Items folder.

Occasionally e-mail can contain viruses, usually as attachments to the e-mail (see page 30). Always make sure you have up-to-date anti-virus software.

More often, you will receive warnings of e-mail viruses, asking you to pass the warning on to everyone you know. Don't panic! These messages are almost always hoaxes. They have no precise date, and can circulate for years. Just delete the message.

Storing messages in folders

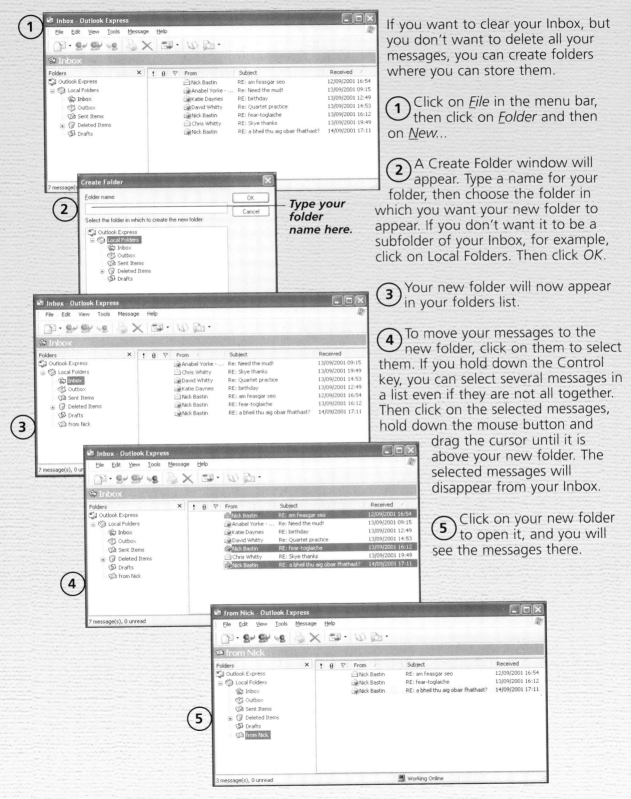

If you want to clear your Inbox, but you don't want to delete all your messages, you can create folders where you can store them.

1 Click on *File* in the menu bar, then click on *Folder* and then on *New...*

2 A Create Folder window will appear. Type a name for your folder, then choose the folder in which you want your new folder to appear. If you don't want it to be a subfolder of your Inbox, for example, click on Local Folders. Then click *OK*.

Type your folder name here.

3 Your new folder will now appear in your folders list.

4 To move your messages to the new folder, click on them to select them. If you hold down the Control key, you can select several messages in a list even if they are not all together. Then click on the selected messages, hold down the mouse button and drag the cursor until it is above your new folder. The selected messages will disappear from your Inbox.

5 Click on your new folder to open it, and you will see the messages there.

Attachments

You can send many different kinds of files with an e-mail message, by "attaching" them to the message. You can attach files you have created in other programs, such as word-processing or spreadsheet files, so that someone else can look at your work. You can also send pictures, music and even video clips, as long as they are in a form which can be stored on your computer.

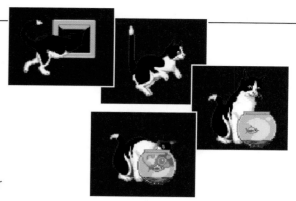

This is an "exe", or executable file. Exe files are programs in themselves. This one will run an animated figure of Felix the cat, which plays on your desktop.

Attaching a file

To attach a file in Outlook® Express, follow the instructions below. Most other e-mail programs work in a similar way.

(1) Open a New Message window and fill in the header as you would normally. Write any message you want to send with the attachment.

(2) Click on the *Attach* button (or paperclip symbol) above the message window, or click on *Insert* in the Menu bar and select *File Attachment...*

(3) An Insert Attachment window will appear. Choose the file you want to insert, and click on it to select it, then click on *Attach*.

(4) A new line will appear in your message header, with details of your attachment.

(5) Click on the *Send* button. Your message and its attachment will be sent as normal.

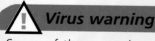

⚠ Virus warning

Some of the most dangerous computer viruses can be spread via attachments to e-mails. Never open an attachment unless it has been sent by someone you know and you are quite sure it is harmless.

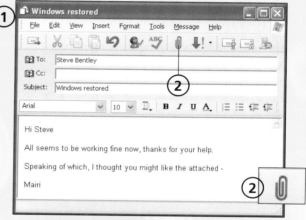

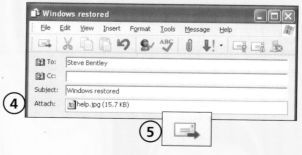

Opening an attachment

When you receive an e-mail with a file attached, it will appear in your Inbox like a normal message, but you will also see a paperclip symbol to the left of the envelope icon.

(1) Double-click on the message to open it as you would normally.

(2) You will see the attachment in a line below the Subject line. Double-click on the name of the attachment to open it.

(3) You will see an Open Attachment Warning window. If you want to open the attachment right away, click on *Open it* and then click *OK*.

(4) If you want to save the attachment and look at it later, click on *Save it to disk*. A Save Attachment As window will appear, and you can choose where you want to keep the attachment on your computer.

Remember, it's best not to open e-mails or attachments from a person you don't know, as they could contain viruses (see page 28).

Large files

If you are sending an attachment with an e-mail, make sure that it is not too big to send. Files over 1MB in size can cause problems.

If you connect to the Internet using an ordinary modem, a large file can take time to send or receive. Some ISPs will not accept large attachments, so if you do have to send a large file, make sure that both your ISP and the ISP of the person you are sending to will accept it.

You may be able to break the file up into several smaller files. Alternatively, you could compress it using a program such as WinZip® (for PCs) or StuffIt™ (for Macintosh computers). You can get copies of these via the Internet (see page 43). If you send a compressed file, make sure that the person you are sending it to has the same program, so that they can decompress the file when they receive it.

Can I send an attachment to anyone?

Not everyone can receive attachments. Some business networks reject all exe files as a matter of course, in case they contain viruses. Exe files created on a PC will generally not work on a Macintosh computer, and vice versa.

Some other files, such as graphics, sound or video files, can only be opened if you have the right software. For video files, this might be RealPlayer® or QuickTime™, both of which are available on the World Wide Web (see page 41).

— 31 —

Mailing lists

You can use e-mail to get in touch with people all over the world who share your interests, simply by joining a mailing list. There are hundreds of thousands of mailing lists covering every subject you could imagine. You can even set up a list of your own.

How do mailing lists work?

There are two main types of mailing list: announcement lists and chat lists.

Announcement lists are usually run by organizations and are used to send out information. For example, a band might use an announcement list to publicize their tours and recordings.

Chat lists are more like newsgroups (see pages 36-39) except that e-mail is sent directly to everyone on the list. One person sends an e-mail to the mailing list itself, and it is then forwarded to all the other people on the list. Many sports teams have mailing lists for fans to discuss recent games.

How do I find out about a list?

The best place to find out about mailing lists is the World Wide Web (find out how to use the Web on pages 38-55). For links to Web sites with directories of mailing lists, go to Usborne Quicklinks at **www.usborne-quicklinks.com**

The **PAML** (Publicly Accessible Mailing Lists) Web site has links to thousands of mailing lists, regularly checked to make sure they are still operating. The easiest way to find a list is to use the index and click on the first letter of the main list subject. For example, click on **m** for music, then click on **music** in the list that appears, then scroll through the next list to find a musical style or group.

This is the Yahoo!® Groups Web site.

Use the directory to find a list subject, or try a search.

The directory site **Yahoo!®** also has a mailing list section, where you can look for a list that you can join. Click on a category in the list directory, and you will be given a list of subcategories. Click on a subcategory, and so on until you find the exact subject you are looking for.

Both PAML and Yahoo! have Search options, where you type in a word (or a few words, for a more precise search) and the search will find related lists for you. For example, if you are looking for mailing lists about basketball, type **Basketball** in the Search box and you might get a selection of lists for coaches, fans and players. If you type **Basketball fans** (**Basketball;fans** on the PAML site) you will get lists for fans only.

How do I join a list?

Joining a mailing list is called subscribing. To subscribe to a list, you send an e-mail to the list itself or to the list moderator (the person who manages the list). If you find out about a list through the PAML or Yahoo! Groups Web sites, the Web site will tell you who you should address your first e-mail to, and what you should put in your message.

Once you have subscribed to a list, you will receive a welcome message telling you more about the list. Keep a copy of this message, as it will tell you how to leave the list, or unsubscribe, if you want to.

Setting up your own list

If you can't find a mailing list for a particular subject, or if you want to keep in touch with a particular group of friends, you may like to set up your own list. A mailing list can be a great way to stay in touch with friends from school or college, for example.

Web sites such as Yahoo! Groups will set up and manage a list for you, free of charge. You can choose whether to make your list public or private: a public list will be included in Yahoo!'s directory, and anyone can choose to join it.

To set up a list, you will need to create a Yahoo! ID and choose a password (find password advice on page 16). Yahoo! gives you full, clear instructions on how to do this, and then on how to start up and run your list.

Tips for using mailing lists

@ Only subscribe to one or two lists at first, otherwise you may receive more e-mail than you can manage.

@ If you have joined a chat list, wait a little while before you send any messages yourself. Read the messages sent to the list for a week, and you will see how the other members communicate, so that you can avoid repeating points that have been made recently.

@ When you reply to a message, include the point you are responding to in the original message. This is called quoting. You can find out how to quote part of a message on page 25. Don't include the whole of the original message, as it will make your reply less easy to read.

@ If a list sends out lots of messages every day, you might ask to be sent a summary of messages once a day or once a week, so that you are not constantly receiving e-mail. This summary is called a digest.

@ Unsubscribe from a list when you are going away, and subscribe again when you get home. Otherwise you may find hundreds of messages waiting for you.

Smileys and shorthand

In an e-mail, it's sometimes hard to tell whether a person is being serious or making a joke. If you want to show that you are joking, you can use a "smiley" or "emoticon" made up of characters on your keyboard. When you look at a smiley sideways, it looks like a face.

There are hundreds of different smileys. Here are a few of them:

 Smiling   Angel

;-) Winking   :-o Surprised

:-D Laughing   <:-) Dumb question

:-(Sad face   :-P Sticking tongue out

:/) Not funny   :*) Clowning around

It's best not to use too many smileys when you are sending a message to a mailing list for the first time, however, as not everyone appreciates them.

To save time typing, some e-mail users have developed acronyms which are abbreviations of often-used phrases. Here are some you might see:

AFAIK As Far As I Know

BTW By The Way

FYI For Your Information

IMHO In My Humble Opinion

LOL Laughing Out Loud

NRN No Reply Necessary

ROFL Rolling On the Floor Laughing

TIA Thanks In Advance

Newsgroups

You can use your e-mail program to join a discussion group, called a newsgroup, and get in touch with people who share your interests. From abstract art to zebras, there are newsgroups covering almost every topic. People discuss very little actual news, it's mostly chat and trivia, but it's fun.

What is a newsgroup?

Messages are sent or "posted" to a newsgroup by members of the group. The messages are stored on a computer, called a news server, maintained by your ISP. Once you have subscribed, or joined a newsgroup, you can read the messages and post new ones of your own.

What software do I need?

The program you need to use newsgroups, called a newsreader, is generally included with the e-mail program supplied with your browser. If you have Microsoft® Windows® 95 or a later version of Windows®, you'll find you have a newsreader built into Outlook® Express.

Newsgroup names

Each newsgroup has a unique name. The name acts as a guide to its theme.

The first part of the name describes the category the group belongs to, such as recreational activities or science. Here are some of the main categories:

comp – computer-related groups
rec – recreational and sports groups
soc – groups which debate social issues such as politics, religion or philosophy
sci – science-related groups
misc – all the groups that don't fit into any other category

Each part of a newsgroup's name narrows down the group's topic area. For example, a newsgroup might be called **rec.music.presley**. This would tell you that the newsgroup is in the recreational activities category, and it is for fans of the music of Elvis Presley.

⚠ Go carefully

As with other areas of the Internet, you'll find lots of good and interesting information in newsgroup discussions, but there are occasional newsgroups and newsgroup users who post offensive material.

Some newsgroups are "moderated", meaning that messages are checked for offensive content before being posted to the group, but most are unmoderated. ISPs generally don't provide access to groups that regularly post unsuitable material, so you shouldn't find them amongst your ISP's list of newsgroups (see opposite).

Unfortunately there is not much to prevent users from posting inappropriate material, although they may be "flamed" (see page 24) by other users if they do. However, you can block the senders of

offensive content (see page 28) and messages from them will not appear on your computer. You can also use Parental Controls in AOL (see page 15) or a filter program (see page 117).

Always remember that newsgroups can be read by anybody, so never include personal information in your messages.

Choose a nickname, rather than giving your real name, when you open your news account (see opposite). You should also be particularly careful about giving your e-mail address, as newsgroups often attract spam (see page 28). To avoid automatically-sent spam, people often insert extra words into their e-mail address. An example might be **mairi@*removethis*.usborne.co.uk**. People sending genuine messages will know that they should delete the ***removethis*** part.

Choosing a newsgroup

Follow these steps to choose and subscribe to a newsgroup.

(1) Open Outlook Express and select *Accounts* in the *Tools* menu.

(2) In the Internet Accounts window, click on the *News* tab. Click on the *Add* button and select *News*.

(3) An Internet Connection Wizard will open and ask you to type in certain information. This includes the name and e-mail address you want your messages to appear from (see "Go carefully" opposite), and the name of your ISP's news server. This usually begins with **news.** followed by your ISP's domain name, but if you are not sure, try looking on the Help or Member Services section of your ISP's Web site, or call your ISP and ask. Finally click on the *Finish* button.

(4) You will see the Internet Accounts window again, with the name of your ISP's news server now appearing in it. Click *Close*.

(5) A window will appear asking you if you want to download a list of your ISP's newsgroups. Click *Yes*. A window will appear telling you that a list of newsgroups is being downloaded. This will take a few minutes as there are many thousands of newsgroups.

(6) A list of newsgroups will appear in the Newsgroup Subscriptions window. To find a group that interests you, type a key word into the "Display newsgroups which contain" box. For example, if you are interested in travel, type **rec** (for recreation) **travel**.

(7) When you find a group you want to subscribe to, click on its name in the list, then click the *Subscribe* button. (Try just one or two at first.) Finally click OK.

Enter your key word or words here.

(8) To see a list of the groups you have subscribed to, click on the name of your ISP's news server in your Folders list.

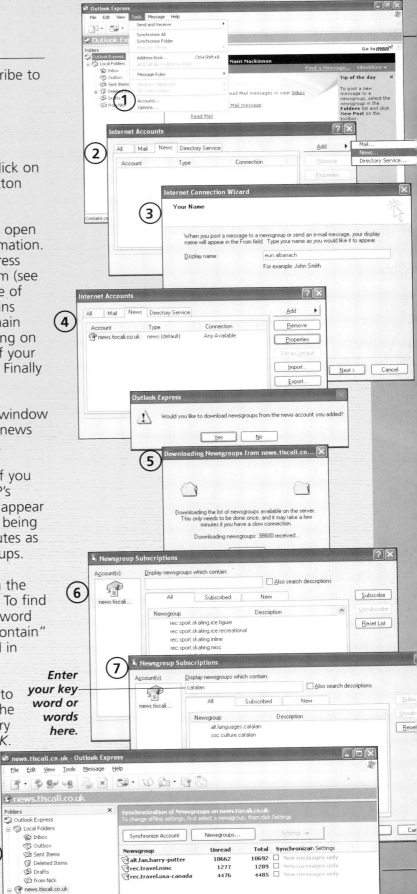

Posting to newsgroups

As a new member of a newsgroup it's fun to get involved in discussions or ask for information and advice. On these pages you'll find out how.

Articles

The messages sent to newsgroups are called articles or postings. Once you have subscribed to a newsgroup, your news server can send you a copy of all the articles that have been posted to that group in the last few days.

Reading articles

To read the articles, you will need to open your newsreader program, in this case Microsoft® Outlook® Express. Double-click on the name of your ISP's news server to display a list of the newsgroups to which you have subscribed.

Double-click on the name of a newsgroup. When you do this for the first time, Outlook Express will download a list of recent articles. This list will appear in the right-hand window. You may also see the beginning of a highlighted article in a preview pane below. To read an article in full, simply double-click on its subject line in the list.

Keeping track

Once you have read an article, your newsreader will mark it as read. In Outlook Express, read articles are shown in normal type, with a whole paper icon, while unread articles are in bold type, with a torn paper icon.

Reading messages offline

If you are paying for your time online, it can be expensive to read through a number of articles while you are connected to the Internet. A better option is to synchronise your newsgroups when you open Outlook Express. This means that Outlook Express can check for new articles in each group, and download them to your computer. You can then read them later, when you are offline.

To do this, click on the name of your news server in your Folders list. A list of the newsgroups to which you have subscribed appears on the right. Click on the name of a newsgroup, then click on the Settings button and select New Messages Only.

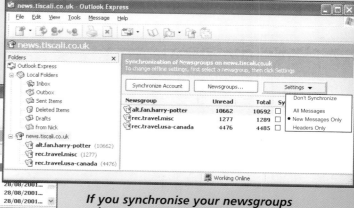

If you synchronise your newsgroups when you open Outlook Express, new messages will be downloaded to your computer and you will be able to read them while you are offline.

Outlook Express showing articles in a newsgroup

Articles with a torn paper icon have not been read.

List of articles

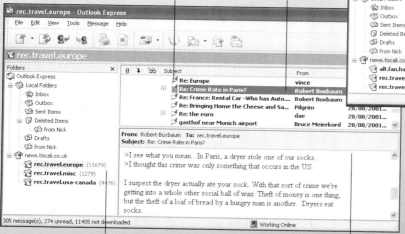

This number shows how many articles are currently in the newsgroup.

The preview pane shows part of an article.

Lurking

When you first join a newsgroup, don't start posting articles right away. Spend a couple of days reading the ones written by other members first, to get an idea of what kind of discussions are currently in progress. This is called lurking.

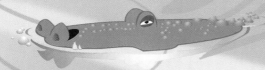

The details of the newsgroup are filled in automatically at the top of the message window.

Give your article a subject.

Type your article here.

Frequently Asked Questions

A Frequently Asked Questions (FAQ) article is a message which contains a list of the questions most often asked by new newsgroup members. It saves other members from having to answer the same questions again and again.

Many newsgroups have a FAQ article which appears every couple of weeks. Look out for it, and read it before you start posting.

Ready to post

After you have lurked for a few days, you will be ready to post your own article. You have two main options – you can start a new discussion, known as starting a new thread, or join in an existing conversation by responding to an article.

Starting a new thread

To start a new thread, open Outlook Express and select a newsgroup from the list of the groups to which you are subscribed. Click the *New Post* button on Outlook's toolbar. A New Message window will appear, with the name of the newsgroup in the *Newsgroups* box at the top of the window.

Type in a title for your article in the *Subject* box, and then type in your message in the message area. When you have finished, click on the *Send* button.

Joining in a discussion

An existing thread consists of an initial message, such as "Ronaldo is the greatest soccer player in history", followed by responses from other members of the newsgroup. The initial message should be displayed in your newsreader with a "+" icon beside it. If you click on this symbol, a list of the articles in the thread will appear. The responses in the thread should have the same subject line with "Re:" in front of it.

To join in, open the message you want to respond to by double-clicking on its Subject line. You have two choices: you can send a message to all the members of the newsgroup (called following up), or just to the person who wrote the article. Either way, it's best to edit the original article so that it contains only the points you are answering (see page 25).

To follow up, click the *Reply Group* button in the toolbar of the window in which the article appears. A New Message window will open, with the details of the newsgroup filled in, and the same subject line as the message you are following up. Type in your article.

To reply directly to the author of an article, click the *Reply* button and type your reply in the New Message window as described above. Your reply will be e-mailed to the author and will not be posted to the group.

The World Wide Web

The World Wide Web, sometimes just called the Web, is probably the most exciting part of the Internet. It is used by organizations and individuals to publish all kinds of information. Millions of people have access to this information, and most of it is free. The Web is huge, and growing all the time.

What can I use it for?

You can use the Web to get news from around the world, events listings, pictures, music and movie previews. You can buy – and sell – anything and everything, from houses to holidays. You can look for detailed information about a particular subject, or you can explore and find things which catch your interest.

What is a Web site?

When you see an address beginning www, or http://www, you can tell that it is the address of a Web site. Web site addresses are called URLs (Uniform Resource Locators).

Information on the Web is displayed on "pages", like those shown below. A Web site may have one or more pages. Most companies have Web sites, where you can find information about the company and perhaps buy their products. Newspapers and magazines publish online versions on their Web sites. Some companies only operate via the Web, offering information, goods or services.

You can find online newspapers, reference sites, museums and art galleries, banks, travel agencies, book and music stores on the Web. There are also some fantastic sites for music and sports fans.

People can also create their own Web sites, to tell other people about themselves or their interests. Sometimes "unofficial" Web sites, created by fans, are just as interesting and attractive as "official" sites. Find out how to create your own Web site on pages 80-109.

How do I get on to the Web?

If you connect to the Internet via an online service, you can get on to the Web simply by typing a URL into the Keyword (or Go word) box at the top of the screen. Otherwise you will need a program called a browser.

The two most widely-used browsers are Microsoft® Internet Explorer and Netscape® Navigator, which is included in the Netscape Communicator package. You may have one or other of these already installed on your computer, or your ISP may have provided you with a copy. Look for the browser icon on your computer desktop, and double-click on this icon to open your browser.

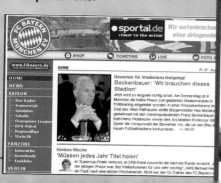

The home page

The first page you will see is your browser's home page – or your ISP's home page, if your browser was supplied by your ISP. Most ISPs' home pages look a little like the front page of a newspaper. You can start exploring the Web from the home page itself, by clicking on pictures or highlighted text.

Web pages and Web sites are connected by a vast network of links called hyperlinks. These take you from one page to another, related page. There are two ways of seeing whether an item

is a hyperlink: if it is in a piece of text, the link itself will usually be in a different colour from the rest of the text and may also be underlined. A picture can also be a hyperlink. With both text and picture links, your mouse cursor will change from an arrow to a pointing hand when it is on top of a link.

Clicking on the link will take you to the linked page, which will start to appear in your browser window in place of the page you were looking at previously.

The main page shown below is the UK home page of an international ISP. The arrows show how text and picture links connect to different pages.

The URL of this site is www.tiscali.co.uk

These are hyperlinks.

Click on a picture or text link to go to the linked page.

Exploring the Web

The Web can be a confusing place, until you know how to get around it. Your browser will help you to explore the Web without getting lost.

Check out a Web site

You can go to any Web site by typing its URL in the Address box (or Netsite box, in Netscape® Navigator) at the top of your browser's window. To get used to using your browser, you could try exploring the NASA Web site. Type the URL **www.nasa.gov** in the Address box, and press the Return key.

This is a browser's toolbar.   ***Type the URL here.***

The NASA home page will start to appear in your browser's window, in place of your browser's or ISP's home page. The page builds up gradually as pictures and text are copied from the NASA server computer to your computer's memory. This process is called downloading. Most Web pages don't take very long to download, but pages with a lot of pictures or animation may take a few minutes.

This is NASA's home page.

Follow the links

You can use the links on this page to find out about the International Space Station. First, find the link "See the Space Station". If it doesn't appear towards the top of the page, scroll down the page by using your mouse to drag the slider bar on the right-hand side. Your mouse will turn into a pointing hand when it is over the link.

Slider bar

Now click on the link. The Human Spaceflight page will start to download. Across the top of the page is a menu: you will see that the items in it are hyperlinks. Click on "Station" in this menu to go to the International Space Station home page.

The International Space Station home page. The same menu appears across the top of all the Human Spaceflight pages.

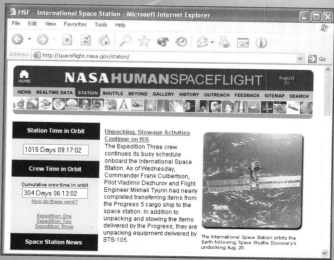

The Back and Forward buttons

When you have finished looking at a page, you may want to go back to the previous page in order to find links to others. You can do this easily by using the *Back* button on your browser, in the top left-hand corner of your browser window. Click on the *Back* button, and the previous page will appear, much more quickly than it did when you first downloaded it. This is because your computer stores a copy of all the pages you download in a browsing session.

Similarly, if you have gone back a page but you decide you would like to see the other page again, you can use the *Forward* button.

The Stop and Refresh buttons

Sometimes you may decide that you do not want to look at a page after all, or you think it is taking too long to download – it may have a lot of picture files, or there may be some problem with the server for that Web site. If you decide that you do not want to wait any longer, click on the *Stop* button. The page will stop downloading, and you can go back to the previous page or type in a different URL.

If you think the page you are looking at is not the most complete or up-to-date version – it may be a version you downloaded at the beginning of a browsing session, or it may not have downloaded all its picture files – you can click on the *Refresh* button to tell your browser to download a new copy of the page.

The Home button

Click on the *Home* button to go back to your browser's (or your ISP's) home page.

You can choose to have a different Web site as your home page, if you like. Find out how to do this on page 51.

Web sites worth seeing

Try browsing around the following sites, and explore some of the many links – you're sure to find something that interests you:

www.bbc.co.uk (the BBC)

www.si.edu (the Smithsonian Institution)

You'll also find direct links to these sites at **www.usborne-quicklinks.com**

These organizations have huge Web sites, with different areas for all kinds of topics.

Type carefully

You must type a URL correctly in order to connect to the right Web site. Be careful with the abbreviations at the end of a domain name – is it ".com" or ".net", ".gov" or ".org"?

If you mis-type a URL you may be connected to a different Web page altogether. More often, you will get an error message like the one below. Check the URL, if you have a record of it, and try typing it again.

The page cannot be displayed

The page you are looking for is currently unavailable. The Web site might be experiencing technical difficulties, or you may need to adjust your browser settings.

This message may mean you have typed the URL incorrectly.

Save it for later

You will soon find that there are Web pages you want to go back to again and again. There are several ways of storing Web pages or URLs so that you can find them quickly.

The History button

Internet Explorer keeps a record of all the Web sites you have visited recently, so if you remember visiting a site but you don't have its URL, you can check your History. Click on the *History* button and a panel, like the one shown on the right, will open on the left-hand side of your browser window.

The History panel shows you the names and URLs of sites you have visited during the past two weeks.

If you click on a site folder, you can see a list of the pages you have visited at that site.

"Favorites"

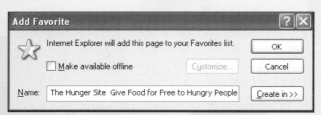

You can instruct your browser to keep a record of sites you want to look at again. Internet Explorer calls these Favorites (in Netscape, they are called Bookmarks).

When you find an interesting site, click on *Favorites* in the menu bar at the top of your browser window, and then on *Add to Favorites...* You will see a message like the one below. Check the name given to the site – you can change it if you want – and click *OK*.

Add Favorite

Internet Explorer will add this page to your Favorites list.

☐ Make available offline

Name: The Hunger Site Give Food for Free to Hungry People

OK
Customize...
Cancel
Create in >>

*Use the **Add to Favorites...** command to keep a record of a site so that you can find it again easily.*

When you want to visit a site in your list of Favorites, just click on the *Favorites* button and then click on the name of the site in the panel.

Organizing your Favorites

In time, you will have a long list of sites. You can use the *Organize...* button at the top of the Favorites panel to sort these into folders, or to delete sites you no longer want. When you click on a site name, you will see its details in the box to the left, including how often you have visited it in the past two weeks.

Organize...

This window shows you details of a site in your Favorites list.

Saving pictures

You might want to save a copy of a picture you find on a Web site. To do this, click on the picture with the right-hand button on your mouse and a menu will appear. Click on *Save Picture As...* and a window will open like the one below.

Use the *Save in:* box to select the folder where you want to save the picture. Use the *File name:* box to choose a name for it and then click on the *Save* button.

Use this window to choose where you want to save a picture, and to give it a file name.

You can then find the picture file in the folder you have selected. Double-click on the file to open it.

These pictures can be found on the Web site of the Louvre museum in Paris. Find a link to this site at www.usborne-quicklinks.com

Saving text

The easiest way to save text from a Web site is to select it with your mouse cursor and copy it into a new file, such as a word processing document. To do this, highlight the text you want to copy and then click on *Edit* in the menu at the top of your browser window, and then *Copy*. Open your new document and click on *Edit* and then *Paste* to insert the text.

Copyright

Most of the information on the Web is available free. This doesn't mean that you can do what you like with it. Information and pictures generally belong to the person who created them, or to an organization representing that person. This is called "intellectual property" or "copyright".

You can save information onto your computer for your personal use, but if you want to publish either pictures or text in any way (including elsewhere on the Web), you must get permission from the person or company that owns the copyright. If you don't do this, you may be breaking the law.

Working offline

You need to be online to download new pages, but if you want to go back through the pages you have downloaded in a browsing session and look at them in more detail, it may be better to work offline. This will save you money on your phone bill, or time if your ISP allows you only a certain amount of connection time free of charge.

Click on *File* in the Menu bar at the top of your browser window, and then click on *Offline* or *Work Offline*. You will see a message asking whether you want to hang up the modem. Click on *Yes*.

To check that you are offline, look for a symbol like one of these at the bottom of your browser window.

These buttons show that you are offline.

Plug-ins

Some Web sites include features, such as sound or animation, which you will only be able to see or hear if you have a particular kind of software installed on your computer. The software is called a "plug-in", and works with your browser to give it extra features.

Where can I find the software?

Sometimes you can find direct links to plug-ins from a Web site. For example, you might click on the link to a video clip. If you do not have the right plug-in on your computer, you may see a link to the site where you can download it. Click on the link, and follow the instructions you are given. Otherwise you can download the plug-ins mentioned on the page opposite via **www.usborne-quicklinks.com**.

If you are asked where on your computer you want to install a plug-in, select the Plug-ins folder in your browser folder, which you will find in your Program Files folder.

⚠ Are plug-ins safe?

If you download any software over the Internet, there is a small risk that you could download a virus or some other element in the software which could damage your computer. Usually you will get a warning message like the one shown below.

Click on Yes *if you are sure you want to continue with the installation.*

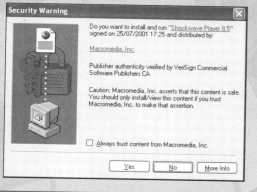

Can I manage without the plug-in?

Different plug-ins work in different ways. Some, such as QuickTime or RealPlayer® (see opposite), are only used for one part of a site, such as a sound or video clip. If you don't have the plug-in, you will not be able to watch or listen to the clip, but you will be able to explore the rest of the site.

Other plug-ins, such as Flash™ animation (see opposite), are an important part of the whole site's design. You may have the choice of looking at a non-animated, non-Flash version of the site, but otherwise you will not be able to see most of the site's contents.

This Flash animation sequence, from the National Geographic Web site, takes you deep into the kelp forest of Monterey Bay, off the California coast.

Barcelona. Catalunya. Spain. U.E.
2° 7' 42" E / 41° 24' 42" N

Java™

One of the most widely-used animation effects is Java. Java is American slang for coffee, and just as coffee makes people more animated, Java can be used to make Web pages look more lively. It is actually not so much a plug-in as a programming language which creates small programs called applets. These might be moving text or small animated figures which can then be inserted in Web pages.

Java is designed to work on all browsers, but early versions of Netscape® and Microsoft® Internet Explorer may not recognize applets. If you have problems with Web pages containing applets, try downloading a more up-to-date version of your browser (for more information on downloading, see pages 46-47).

Flash™

Flash animation is used to create fast-moving animated text and images which can make sites look spectacular. Flash sites generally download and run quickly and smoothly, and the images are clearer than other kinds of animation. Many official band sites, as well as official sites for the latest films, use Flash.

Watch as the camera pans around the harbour and night turns to day on the MyCity Web site for Barcelona

RealPlayer®

If you want to listen to music on the Internet, you will need a plug-in. Most online music stores and radio stations use a process called RealAudio® to put music clips on their Web sites, and to play RealAudio clips you will need RealPlayer. RealPlayer also includes RealVideo®, which is used by television network sites for video clips, and also for movie previews and Webcasts (see page 59).

Other popular plug-ins for listening to music online include MP3 players. You can find out more about MP3 on page 59.

Shockwave®

Shockwave is used to create interactive sites, which are especially good for games. On an interactive site you make things happen by moving or clicking your mouse – you can make characters move, or turn objects around, or explore a virtual area, or choose and play sound or video clips. Shockwave allows you to look at sites containing animation, video and sound, which can all be played together in one file.

These figures are part of a game on the MyCity Web site for London.

QuickTime

QuickTime is another plug-in which is used to play video clips. It also includes QTVR (QuickTime Virtual Reality), which can be used to show 360° views, for example on a tour of a building. You can click on an image and move it around or zoom in and out, as though you were controlling a video camera. Find out more about virtual reality on pages 70-71.

Web sites for plug-ins

You can find links to the Web sites where you can download all the plug-ins mentioned on this page at **www.usborne-quicklinks.com**

You'll also find links to the MyCity sites, where you can see examples of Flash and Shockwave in action.

RealPlayer is a trademark of Real Networks, Inc., registered in the US and other countries.
QuickTime is a trademark of Apple Computer, Inc., registered in the US and other countries.
Flash and Shockwave are trademarks of Macromedia, Inc., registered in the US and other countries.

Downloading programs

You can find lots of sites on the Web offering software for you to download, or copy on to your computer. Software downloads might include programs to help you use the Internet more efficiently, programs to help you at work and games programs. Many of these are available free of charge.

Looking for software

A good place to start looking for software on the Internet is your browser's or your software manufacturer's home page. You might find useful plug-ins (see page 44), or an updated version of your browser.

There are also a number of sites which have lists of links to downloads, news and reviews of new programs. Some of these are listed in the box on the page opposite.

Downloading a program

When you have found the software you want, you may be asked to type in your name and e-mail address. You should say which operating system you are using, Windows® or Macintosh. Most software available for downloading requires Windows® 95 or a later version, or MacOS 8.5 or a later version. If you are not sure that you have the right operating system, look for a link to System requirements, click on it and check. Once you have given all the necessary information, click on the Download link. A window will appear like the one below.

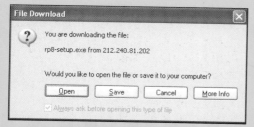

A window like this one will appear when you start to download a file. Choose the option Save or Save this program to disk.

Saving a program

Select the option *Save* or *Save this program to disk*, and click on OK. Another window will appear, allowing you to choose where you want to save the software you are downloading.

The Save As window

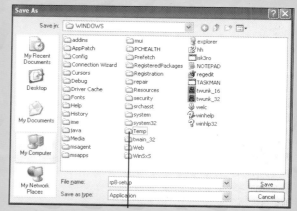

Double-click on this folder to open it.

Double-click on the Temp folder (on a PC, you may find it in your Windows folder in My Computer), then click on *Save*. You will see a window showing you how your download is progressing. When this window tells you the download is complete, close it.

Installing a program

Close down any other programs you have running. Double-click on the My Computer icon on your desktop, and go to the Temp folder.

You should see a new icon with a file name ending .exe. Double-click on this icon and then follow the instructions you are given. You will be shown an "End User License Agreement", by which you agree not to modify or copy the software unlawfully. Click on "I accept" to continue with the installation. Finally, you may be asked to restart your computer.

If the program was compressed (see opposite), the filename will have a different ending, and you will need the same compression software to extract a full-sized version of the file. Double-click on the file to decompress it, and then move it to your Program Files folder.

How much does the software cost?

Some of the software available on the Web is free. For other software, you may have to pay before you can download it. It should cost no more than if you bought the same product in a store, and there are many excellent programs which cost very little.

 Freeware This is software which is free for anyone to copy onto their computer and use. Sometimes it is a basic version of a program, and you can pay extra for the complete version.

 Shareware You can download this software and try it for free. By doing this, you accept certain conditions. A common condition is that you will pay a small charge for a program if you decide to keep using it after an initial trial period of 30 days. You will then be registered to use the program, and you may be offered a fuller version of the program or free upgrades.

 Trialware You can try out this software for free, but it contains a device which prevents you from using it fully. Some programs have features which don't work. Others contain a built-in timer which stops the whole program from working after an initial trial period. If you decide to keep the program, you pay the company who developed it. They will send you a registration number. This is a code which makes the program work properly.

 Alphaware/Betaware This is new software that needs to be tested. Alphaware is a very early version of a program, and it is generally too risky to try unless you are an experienced computer user. Betaware may still have one or two minor faults, and if you find a fault in a beta program, you should tell the company that created it.

Compressed files

Large program files can take a long time to download, so files are often compressed to take up less space (and less downloading time). You need special software to create a compressed file. You also need the same software to create a full-sized file from a compressed file, before your computer can open the file and run the program. When you have created the full-sized file, you can delete the compressed version.

Compression programs are often available to download via the Internet as shareware or trialware. You can find links to the Web sites of some of the best-known at **www.usborne-quicklinks.com**

Sites with software to download

Find direct links to these sites at **www.usborne-quicklinks.com**

You can start looking for useful downloads on the **Microsoft® Internet Explorer**, **Netscape®** and **Apple** Web sites.

The **Tucows** and **CNet Shareware** Web sites have links to downloads, and search facilities to help you find particular products.

If you're looking for compression software, try the Web sites of **WinZip®** (for PCs) and **StuffIt™** (for Macintosh computers).

⚠ Be careful

Always remember that when you download software via the Internet, there is a risk that you could download a virus or some other element in the program which might damage your computer. If you use a computer at school or at work, always ask your system administrator before downloading any software.

Searching the Web

There is a huge amount of information available on the Web, but it can be hard to know where to look for something in particular. However, there are services available on the Web to help you find information. These services are called search engines. Search engines work in two main ways: as directories or as indexes.

Directories

Web directories are run by large organizations which collect information about Web sites and arrange them in categories and sub-categories. Categories are connected by hyperlinks, so that you can go from one to the next, making your search more and more precise until you have a short list of relevant sites.

This is Yahoo!'s home page.

Yahoo!® is one well-known directory. You might use it, for example, to look for information on the city of Barcelona. Firstly, type Yahoo!'s URL into your browser's address box. You will see Yahoo!'s home page, as shown below.

Click on the Countries link, in the Regional section to download a page with an index of countries. Click on Spain, and you will download another page with a short list of country subjects. Click on Cities to download an index of towns and cities, and finally click on Barcelona in this index. You will download a page of links covering different areas of interest.

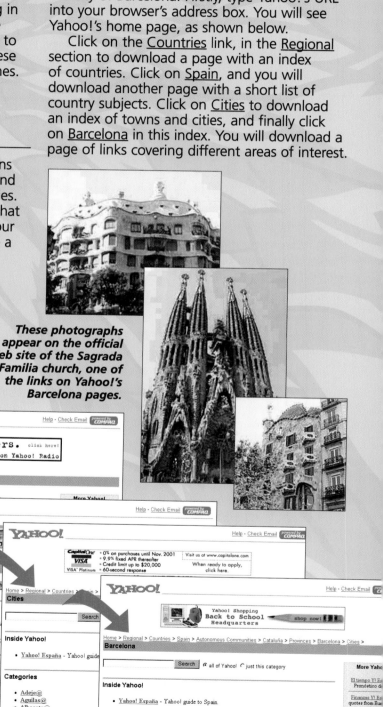

These photographs appear on the official Web site of the Sagrada Familia church, one of the links on Yahoo!'s Barcelona pages.

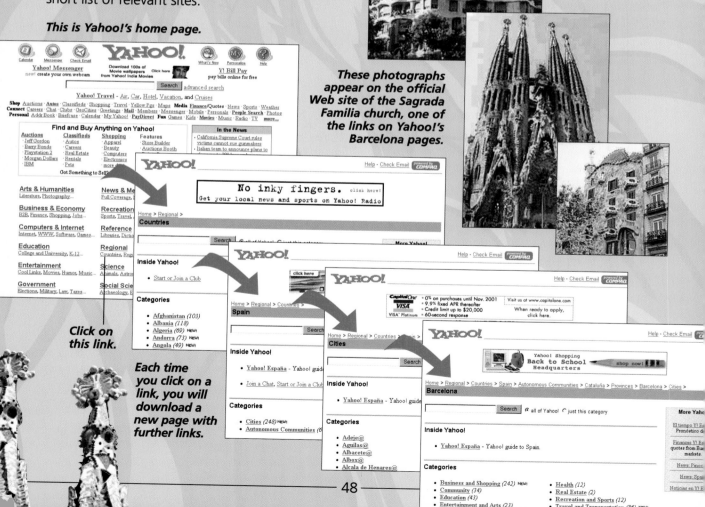

Click on this link.

Each time you click on a link, you will download a new page with further links.

These are some pictures of volcanoes found through a Yahoo! search.

Word searches

If you are looking for information but you are not sure which categories to look in, you could try typing a word or a few words in the Search box at the top of the page. For example, if you want to find out about volcanoes, type **volcanoes** in the Search box.

This is Yahoo!'s UK home page. Directories like Yahoo! often have pages for different countries around the world. This makes it easy to find sites created in your home country or in your own language.

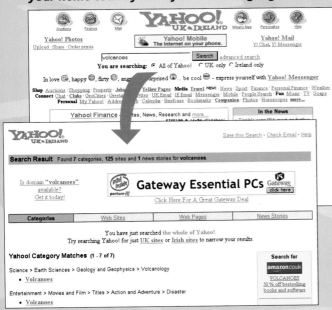

The results of a search for "volcanoes"

Yahoo! will look for any current news articles, categories in its own directory, and links to Web sites that relate to volcanoes.

If you want to make a search more precise, type one or two words related to your search subject in the Search box. For example, if you want to find out only about volcanoes in Europe, type **volcanoes europe** in the Search box, and Yahoo! will look for sites which contain both terms.

Are all Web sites in the directory?

There are currently over one billion pages on the Web, and so many new sites are being created every day that it is impossible for any directory to list them all. If you can't find the information you are looking for in one directory, try another. If you still have no luck, try an index (see pages 50-51) or a metasearcher (see pages 52-53).

Missing links

Sometimes Web pages change URLs, and sometimes they are taken off the Web altogether. Directories list so many Web sites that it is impossible for their organizations to keep checking the URLs.

If a site's URL has changed, you may be redirected to the new site automatically, or you may get a message giving the new URL. If the site does not exist any more, you will get an error message. You could try the site again later, in case it is just experiencing a temporary problem with its server. Otherwise, try another directory or an index to see if you can find a more up-to-date URL.

Useful directories

Find direct links to these sites at
www.usborne-quicklinks.com

Yahoo!® is the biggest and most popular directory, with local pages for the US, the UK and countries around the world. It also offers other services such as e-mail, Web site hosting and many more.

LooksmartSM is another popular directory with local pages for different countries.

Most indexes (see next page) include directory sections on their opening pages which work in a similar way to the above.

Indexes

Indexes are the most effective way of looking for a particular word or phrase in a Web site's name or on the site itself.

How do they work?

An index is a program which explores the Web, finding new sites and adding them to its own enormous list of pages. When you use an index, it will scan the list for words matching your search and show you a number of results or "hits" in order of how closely they seem to match.

For example, you might look for a virtual tour of a city by typing "virtual tour" and the city name in the Search box, then clicking on Search. Below you will see an example from a popular index called Google^SM.

This is Google's home page.

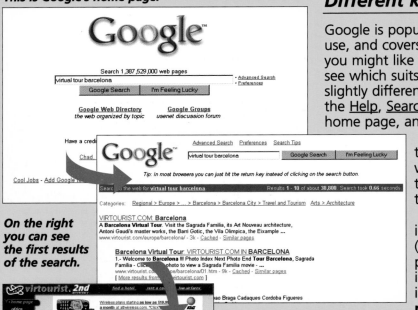

On the right you can see the first results of the search.

If you're pretty sure Google will find the Web site you want, click on "I'm feeling lucky" to go directly to the site of the first hit.

Search results

Each item in an index's list of results has a hyperlink to a Web page, and also a little information about the page. The first few entries in the results list will match your search quite closely, but the further down the list you read, the less relevant the links are likely to be.

The best match will be the site which includes all your search terms in its title or description (the information the site gives directly to search engines), or together in one phrase on the page. Indexes also have a system of ranking sites, so that the most popular or established appear higher up the results list. Your search may return thousands of hits – but don't worry, you'll probably find what you want near the top of the list.

Different kinds of index

Google is popular because it is fast and easy to use, and covers a huge number of sites, but you might like to try a few other indexes and see which suits you best. They may work in slightly different ways; for best results look for the Help, Search Help or Search Tips link on the home page, and follow the advice there.

With all indexes, it's essential to spell words correctly. Indexes will match the exact word you type in the Search box, so be sure to type accurately.

If you use capital letters, as in **Guitar Music**, most indexes (except Google) will only find pages which use capital letters in the same places. If you don't include capitals, as in **guitar music**, indexes will find pages whether they use capitals or not, giving you many more results.

With some indexes (though not Google), you can use an asterisk* at the end of a word to look for the same word with different endings. If you type **photograph***, for example, the index will also find pages which mention photographs, photography, photographers and so on.

Smart searching

To help you to filter out links to irrelevant Web pages, indexes have tools to make a search more precise.

If you are looking for a particular phrase, you can put it in inverted commas: **"emperor penguins"** will find pages which mention emperor penguins rather than any other kind of penguin – or indeed any other kind of emperor.

Using operators

You can use shorthand instructions called operators to make your search more specific. Different indexes use different operators, so check the Help, Search Help or Search Tips link on the home page. However, most indexes recognize the operators **+** (and) and **–** (not).

 If you want to search for sites which include several particular terms, not necessarily in the same phrase, type a plus sign before each word in the Search box. For example, if you want to find out about the Vikings in North America, type **+vikings +america** in the Search box. The index will only find pages which include both terms. The more terms you specify, the more precise your search will be.

You can also exclude terms by typing a minus sign before a word. For example, if you are looking for guitar music but you are not interested in classical music, you would type **+guitar +music -classical**.

⚠️ Is it what you want?

Always read the description of a site before you click on the link to it in an index. Because the hits are found by programs rather than people, they occasionally pick up misleading or inaccurate pointers from the site itself.

This is AltaVista®, another popular index, with the first few results of a search.

Indexes

Find direct links to all these sites at **www.usborne-quicklinks.com**

Google[SM] is one of the most popular search engines, super-fast and effective. It operates worldwide, but you can refine your search to return only sites in a particular language.

AltaVista®, **Excite**[SM] and **Lycos®** have local sites for countries around the world, as well as useful directories and other services such as Web-based e-mail on their home pages. AltaVista has a useful Family Filter option to help you exclude sites which might have offensive content from your results list.

Expert searching

If you don't find exactly what you are looking for with a directory or an index, there are a number of Web sites and programs which can help you to search a wider selection of sites, or else to make your search more focused.

Metasearchers

Metasearchers are search engines which search search engines, giving you the best matches from perhaps a dozen sources. They will only retrieve the first few results from any source, giving you fast results which don't include hundreds of irrelevant sites, and they will not include duplicate results from different sources.

One well-known metasearcher on the Web is ixquick. Below you can see the results of a search for information on the Republic of Georgia in Central Asia. Unlike most indexes, this search did not return numbers of unwanted hits for the state of Georgia in the USA.

The Search Results window in ixquick

Map of the Republic of Georgia, found on the Internet

Ask a question

Sometimes you will get better results if you phrase your search as a question. One search engine which lets you do this is Ask Jeeves™.

Ask Jeeves is available in English and Spanish.

The pages above show the results of a search on the Spanish Ask Jeeves site.

You can look at questions other users have asked about particular subjects, to give you an idea how to phrase your question. You can also see questions being asked by other users while you are visiting the site. Once you have keyed in your own question, Ask Jeeves will try a number of search engines to find answers for you.

*Pictures of
the Republic of Georgia found
on the Georgian Parliament's Web site*

Metasearch software

Metasearchers on the Web give impressive results, but there are even more powerful search agents available as software. You can find a program called Copernic® on the Web and install the basic version on your computer free of charge. (See pages 46-47 for information on downloading software.) Macintosh operating system 8.5 and later versions include the search agent Sherlock, which works in a similar way to Copernic.

This window shows the results of a search using Copernic. If you click on a result, you can see a preview of the Web site in question in the bottom left-hand corner of the window.

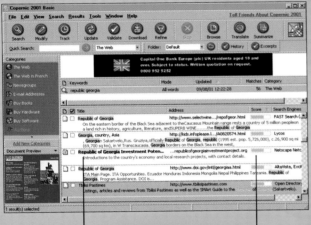

These are the first few results of the search, with the search terms highlighted.

This bar shows the hit's relevance as a percentage.

Copernic and Sherlock not only search a number of search engines at once, they also assess hits for relevance – how closely they relate to the search terms. This is based on whether the search terms are included in the Web page's title or description, or appear near the top of the page, close together or several times on the page. Relevance is given as a percentage in a bar reading.

Looking for anything in particular?

Some search engines specialize in particular kinds of searches – finding news articles, for example, or images or MP3 files. You can save time and find many more of the results you want by using a focused search like this.

Web rings

Web rings are groups of sites with a similar theme. The person or organization which created a Web site agrees to join a ring, and each site in a ring contains links to all the other sites. Yahoo!® has a directory of thousands of Web rings arranged by category, so you can browse the directory to find sites which match your interests.

Search agent sites

Find direct links to these sites at
www.usborne-quicklinks.com

ixquick claims to be the world's most powerful metasearch engine, and its uncluttered design makes it easy to use.

Ask Jeeves™, the question and answer site, also has a good kids' section.

Copernic® basic version can be downloaded free of charge from the Copernic Web site. **Sherlock** is included in the Macintosh operating system, and you can find out more about it on the **Apple** Web site.

Google℠ has a specialist search service for Macintosh-related sites. **AltaVista®** has an image search and **Lycos** will find MP3 files. **ixquick** will search for MP3s, images or news articles.

You can find a list of Web ring topics in the **Yahoo!® WebRing** directory.

Portals, hubs and communities

If you often look for information on the Internet, there are some sites you will visit over and over again, either to find information on the site itself or to be directed to other sites where you will find what you are looking for. A site which you visit a number of times can be called a "portal", a "hub" or a "community". You can find direct links to all the sites on these pages at **www.usborne-quicklinks.com**

What is a portal?

A portal is a Web site which acts as a gateway to other Web sites. All directories and indexes are portals, because you use them in order to find and connect to other Web sites. ISP home pages can also act as portals if they have links to other organizations' news, information and shopping sites.

There are also a number of specialist portals, which have lots of links to "partner sites" related to a particular subject, such as music. These are sometimes called "vertical portals" or "vortals".

What is a hub?

There are some sites which you visit mainly for the up-to-date information you find on the site itself. These sites are known as hubs, and might include news sites (see pages 58-59) and online magazines, as well as sites which tell you about current developments on the Internet.

On CNet's Web site you can find news and reviews of the latest Internet technology.

Sportal is a vertical portal dedicated to sports. It has different sites for countries around the world.

Click on the Shopping link to go to sites where you can buy sports gear.

One of Sportal's partner sites is the Benetton Formula 1 motor racing site.

Community sites

Portals and hubs aim to attract lots of regular visitors. One way to do this is to give visitors the chance to say what they think, via e-mail or forums, also called bulletin boards. A bulletin board is a section of a Web site where visitors can post messages about a particular subject for other visitors to read.

Web sites which encourage visitors to have their say are known as communities. Some community sites will check messages before they are posted to make sure they are not rude or offensive. To post a message, you may have to register with the community site and choose a username and password. As always on the Internet, you should never give out personal information in a message that anyone can read.

The Guardian Unlimited Web site, Virgin.net and the BBC News site all have lively forums to discuss current news and other popular topics.

Changing your home page

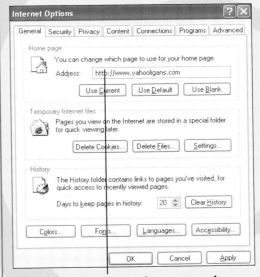

If you visit a particular Web site often, you may like to select it as your home page so that you go directly to that site every time you open your browser. If you are interested in keeping up with the news, for example, you might choose an online newspaper as your home page.

To change your home page in Microsoft® Internet Explorer, click on *Tools* in the Menu bar at the top of your browser window, then click on *Internet Options...* You should see a window like the one below.

The Internet Options window

Type the URL of your chosen page here.

Type the URL of the Web site you would like as your new home page in the *Address* box, and then click on *OK* at the bottom of the window. When you click on the *Home* button in your browser's Toolbar, the page you have selected will appear, and when you reopen your browser, it will open onto this page as your home page.

The World Wide Web is a brilliant place for finding information about almost any subject under the sun. You'll find amazing Web sites bringing history to life, virtual expeditions to the ends of the earth, fact-packed dictionaries and easy-to-use encyclopedias.

On these two pages you'll see some of the best information and learning sites on the Internet. You'll find direct links to all the sites at **www.usborne-quicklinks.com**

Wide World Web

You can explore the world and the universe, from the deepest ocean to furthest known galaxies, all from your own computer. The Web pages shown below are taken from sites with vast and fascinating archives. You can use their powerful search facilities to find out about a particular topic, or just browse until you find something amazing.

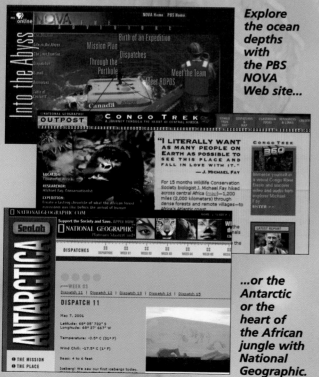

Explore the ocean depths with the PBS NOVA Web site...

...or the Antarctic or the heart of the African jungle with National Geographic.

Wild things

You'll find every kind of creature on the Internet, from prehistoric monsters to popular pets. Look out for stunning photo galleries and live zoocams (Webcams in zoos – find out more about Webcams on page 73). On Web sites about dinosaurs you can often find fantastic reconstructions of the prehistoric world, too.

Wild Web sites: below, an Italian site for animal lovers

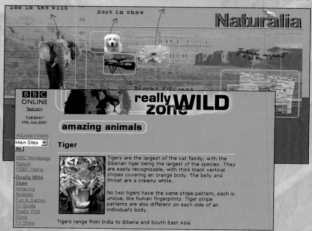

At the BBC's Really Wild Zone you'll find an A-Z of amazing animals.

You can bring prehistory to life on the Discovery Channel Web site, "When Dinosaurs Roamed America".

Days to remember

The Internet is a treasure trove of historical facts, too. As well as the sites featured on this page, you'll find the past brought to life on many Web sites created by museums (find more of these on pages 62-63).

Read first-hand reports of historical events at the Eyewitness Web site, or find out what happened on this day in history on the History Channel's site.

Science made simple

You can find the answer to all kinds of scientific questions on the Internet. Great graphics can make complicated scientific concepts easy to understand – perfect for homework help, or just finding things out for fun.

The Chemistry section of the Sprocketworks Web site has some excellent animated guides, while the How Stuff Works Web site takes the mystery out of anything from ballpoint pens to time travel.

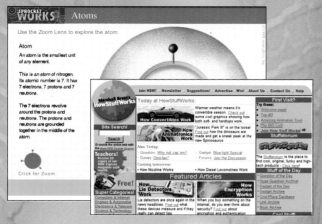

General reference

You'll find answers to every kind of question in an online encyclopedia. You can use some encyclopedias free of charge; others will allow you to try a sample search, but you will have to pay a small charge each month to use the service in full.

Online encyclopedias: the Encyclopædia Britannica and the French Quid.

Web sites for reference

Find direct links to all these sites at
www.usborne-quicklinks.com

The **PBS** Web site, including **NOVA**, covers a vast range of subjects, from ancient history to cybercrime.

The **National Geographic** and the **Discovery Channel** Web sites explore the world and its creatures, from prehistory to the present day, with fascinating reports and spectacular pictures.

The enormous **BBC** Web site isn't just for news. There are excellent sub-sites for history, nature and science, too.

Useful online encyclopedias include the **Encyclopædia Britannica** and Microsoft's **Encarta**, while **xrefer** can search over 50 dictionaries and other reference titles.

News on the Internet

The Internet is an excellent place to find up-to-date news. Most national newspapers have online versions, which you can look at free of charge. Television news networks also have their own Web sites, and you can often find out more about the background of news stories which interest you.

You'll find direct links to all the news sites on these pages at **www.usborne-quicklinks.com**

Online newspapers

Some of the world's most famous newspapers are available online. You can read the latest news reports, or search the archives for previously published articles.

The online versions of the Times in London and the International Herald Tribune

The UK's Guardian Unlimited has links to pages of sports news and movie previews, as well as a useful Web guide.

Above, Le Monde and Gazeta, online newspapers from France and Russia

A translation service

Around 96% of material on the World Wide Web is in English, but if you want to visit sites in other languages, you may find the Babel Fish translation service from AltaVista® useful. Use it to translate a piece of text or a Web site from and into nine languages in seconds. Text is translated word by word, so it may sound a little strange, but you should be able to understand the gist of the original.

Translate foreign-language texts and Web sites in moments with AltaVista's translation service.

Television networks

You will also find in-depth news coverage at the Web sites of television networks such as ITN and CNN. You may be able to listen to sound clips or watch video footage, or have the latest headlines e-mailed to you as the news breaks or at a time you choose.

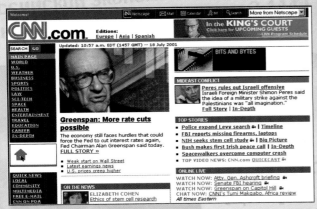

On television network sites such as CNN's, you can play video clips of recent news stories.

The BBC Web site has news pages in English, Welsh, Spanish, Russian, Arabic or Chinese.

The very latest news

Some online newspapers have a special page for "breaking news" – the latest news stories, which usually come from international news agencies such as AFP. You can also visit the news agencies' own Web sites.

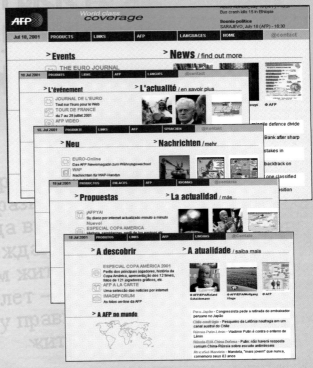

The news agency AFP has news pages in English, French, German, Spanish and Portuguese.

News Web sites

Find direct links to all these sites at **www.usborne-quicklinks.com**

Most national newspapers have online editions – try **The Times**, **The Guardian**, **The New York Times** or **The Washington Post**.

Television news sites include **CNN**, the **BBC** and **ITN**.

You'll find breaking news at the sites of the news agencies **Reuters** and **AFP**.

Times and places

As well as news and reference sites, you can look up all sorts of other useful information on the Internet. You can find out about events in your area and book tickets online, then see how to get to an event with detailed maps and travel information for cities and countries around the world.

You can find direct links to all the sites on these pages at **www.usborne-quicklinks.com**

Events guides

Look at an online events guide for details of special days out, music, movies, theatre, exhibitions, restaurants and shopping. Some guides also include an online booking service, so that you can buy tickets right away for events which catch your eye.

These are guides for London, Paris and New York.

The Time Out Web site features events guides to over 30 cities around the world.

Cinema guides

You can use the Web to read about current movie releases, see trailers, read reviews and find out what's on in your area.

At the Moviefone Web site you can read all about the latest releases. In the US, you can also find details of what's showing in your area, check screening times and also book tickets online for some venues.

Listings Web sites

Find direct links to all these sites at **www.usborne-quicklinks.com**

You'll find events listings for cities around the world on the **Time Out** Web site. **Thisislondon** has news, listings and reviews for the London area, and good visitors' guides to the city, too.

You can buy tickets online for major concerts, theatre and sports events in the US and the UK on the **Ticketmaster** Web sites.

Find out about every film ever made on the massive **Internet Movie Database**, or look up listings for current releases at **moviefone.com**

Maps

Some listings sites include links to street maps of the area around a venue. Specialist map sites offer large-scale and more detailed maps, and even directions for driving to a place on the map.

MapQuest's Web site will find any place in the US or the UK for you, and then tell you how to get there.

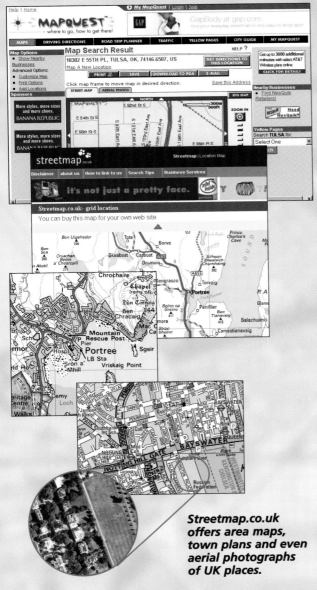

Streetmap.co.uk offers area maps, town plans and even aerial photographs of UK places.

Maps and transport Web sites

Find direct links to all these sites at
www.usborne-quicklinks.com

You'll find UK area maps, street maps and aerial photographs – see if there is one for your area – on **streetmap.co.uk**'s Web site. **MapQuest**'s site has maps for both the US and the UK, with local information and driving directions. There are Paris maps, and subway plans for cities around the world, at the Parisian transport authority **RATP**'s Web site.

Find rail timetables for the UK on the **Railtrack** Web site, or for the US on the **Amtrak** site. **Die Bahn** has European timetables.

Timetables

Once you know where you are going, you can find out how to get there with an online timetable. You can find online timetables for most airlines and national rail networks.

On the Die Bahn Web site for the German railway, you can find train times for destinations across Europe: below, the quickest rail route from Paris to Moscow. (The site is also available in English.)

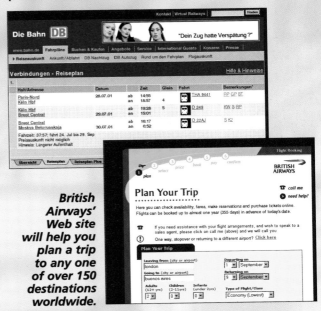

British Airways' Web site will help you plan a trip to any one of over 150 destinations worldwide.

Museums and galleries

Some of the most attractive sites on the Internet have been created by museums and art galleries around the world. You can explore their collections and look at items in detail, or find out more about a subject or an artist. You can find direct links to all the sites on these pages at **www.usborne-quicklinks.com**

The world around us

You can find out about all things animal, vegetable or mineral at natural history museum Web sites from around the world.

The page below gives details of an exhibition at the Museum of Natural History in Paris.

The American Museum of Natural History also has a great junior activity page, "Ology".

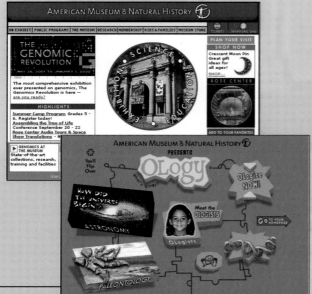

A piece of history

You can visit history museums and explore historic buildings around the world online.

Explore the palace and grounds of Versailles, and meet some of its more famous inhabitants at the Château de Versailles Web site, in English, French or Spanish.

Look at amazing artefacts from around the world on the British Museum's Web site.

Museum Web sites

Find direct links to all these sites at **www.usborne-quicklinks.com**

The **American Museum of Natural History** and the **Natural History Museum, London** both have excellent Web sites.

Great sites for bringing history to life include the **Imperial War Museum** Web sites, linked to museums around the UK, and the **Chicago Museum of Science and Industry**, where you can take a virtual tour of a World War Two submarine, a classic Thirties train or a modern coal mine.

In the picture

Many world-famous art galleries have Web sites where you can take a tour of the picture collections, look at pictures in detail, find out about the artists, see details of exhibitions and even visit the gallery shop. Information is usually available in English and other languages.

A selection of Web sites from art galleries around the world

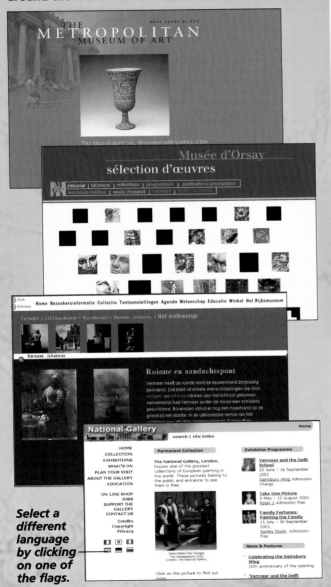

Select a different language by clicking on one of the flags.

Art gallery Web sites

Find direct links to all these sites at **www.usborne-quicklinks.com**

Famous art museums in the UK include London's **National Gallery** and **Tate Gallery**. Both have amazing Web sites.

In the US, Web sites not to be missed include the **Metropolitan Museum** and the **Museum of Modern Art** in New York.

Paris's **Louvre** museum, **Musée d'Orsay** and **Centre Georges Pompidou** have Web sites well worth a visit, as do the **Rijksmuseum** and the **Van Gogh Museum** of Amsterdam.

And the **State Hermitage Museum** of St. Petersburg in Russia has an incredible collection of over three million items, many of which can be seen on its Web site.

Buy gifts online from the museum store at the Web site of the Guggenheim museum in Bilbao.

You can send e-cards (e-mail postcards) from the Web site of the Museum of Modern Art in New York.

Music on the Internet

Whether you are looking for news of a band you like, advice on buying a new guitar or music to download and listen to, you can find it all on the Internet.

You can find direct links to all the sites on these pages at **www.usborne-quicklinks.com**

Online music magazines

Many famous music magazines have Web sites packed with news, reviews and sound clips, as well as links to bands' official and unofficial sites. If you like what you hear, you will find links to online music stores where you can buy CDs, DVDs and videos. (See pages 66-67 for more about online shopping.)

This is the home page of the UK music magazine NME.

The Ultimate Band List on Artist Direct's Web site has news articles and links to official and unofficial sites for around 100,000 bands and artists.

Your own band

If you play in a band yourself, you will find masses of reviews and discussions of instruments and equipment, as well as links to manufacturers' Web sites, at Harmony Central. There are even pages of advice on starting out as a band, including getting gigs and recording.

Harmony Central's home page

Listen to live radio with the WindowsMedia Web site: click on Launch Radio Tuner and select a station.

Online radio

Many radio stations broadcast on the Internet, using a process called "streaming". This means that the sound plays directly as your computer receives the data, and the information is not stored on your computer. Streaming technology is often used for sound and video clips, and you may need to download a plug-in such as RealPlayer® to watch or listen to them. (For more about downloading programs, see pages 46-47.)

What is MP3?

Streaming technology (see opposite) is useful when you want to listen to sound clips or radio channels immediately, but the sound quality is not as good as a CD and you can't save copies of what you are listening to. Storing CD-quality sound on a computer takes a lot of memory space, but it is possible to compress files so that they take up very little space without losing much sound quality.

The most popular compressed sound files are MP3 files. You can download MP3 files and play them on your computer using a special player (you can download the player from the MP3 Web site). You can also use a portable MP3 player. This is a little like a personal stereo, but instead of cassettes or CDs it uses a memory card. You download MP3 tracks from your computer to the player's memory card. If you like the tracks, you can make a permanent copy on CD.

A portable MP3 player

There are several official MP3 sites where you'll find music, mostly by new bands, available to download for free. Established artists also release MP3 tracks from time to time on these sites or their own Web sites.

Copyright

Always remember that music is subject to copyright (see page 43). If you make a permanent copy without permission from the copyright holders, you are breaking the law. Several authorized MP3 sites, such as the MP3 Web site and the sites of some record labels, offer "copyright-free" tracks for you to download. Make sure that you only copy tracks from authorized sites, and that the site states clearly that you have permission to download the tracks you choose.

Neil Barnes, from the band Leftfield, in a Webcast from Brixton Academy in London.

Webcasts

Sometimes bands will broadcast a concert on the Internet. This is called a Webcast. The concert is filmed and recorded, then shown on a Web site using RealAudio® (see page 45) or a similar process. Check online music magazines to find details of any Webcasts coming up.

Music Web sites

Find direct links to all these sites at **www.usborne-quicklinks.com**

For a superb reference guide to all kinds of music, try the **All Music Guide** Web site.

For information about bands, visit the **Artist Direct** Web site, which includes the **Ultimate Band List**. You'll also find band news and links on sites such as **MTV** and **NME**. For direct links to hundreds of artists' official Web sites (often including audio and video clips), try record companies such as **Sony Music**.

For the RealPlayer® plug-in, visit **real.com**. For the MP3 player, go to **mp3.com**, where you'll also find thousands of MP3 tracks to download free of charge. Another great site for MP3 tracks by up-and-coming artists is **peoplesound.com**

Shopping online

You can buy and sell all kinds of things over the Internet, from books to houses.

Although you may not be able to look at goods or try them out before you buy, shopping sites have lots of ways of giving you information about their products, from customer reviews to 3-D images.

On most shopping sites, you pay for goods online, using a credit card. If you are under 18, or don't have a credit card, you may have to ask someone else to buy goods for you.

You can find direct links to all the sites on these pages at **www.usborne-quicklinks.com**

Extracts and sample tracks

Some of the largest online stores are book and music stores. An online store can offer hundreds of thousands of titles, with recommendations, news and reviews and interviews with authors and artists. You can download extracts to read from new books, or play samples of album tracks using a plug-in such as RealPlayer® (see page 45). If you select one title, the store may suggest other similar titles you might enjoy.

MVC is a network of online book, music, video, DVD and games stores in the UK.

Shop around

One of the best things about shopping on the Internet is that it's easy to shop around for the best deal – you can even find Web sites which do exactly that, using software called "shopbots" to visit different online stores and compare prices, including postage and packing which can be an unexpected extra.

Once you have found the best price, you can click on the link to the site it came from and buy the item there. You will get the best results with items like CDs, where the same CD can be sold on different sites for very different prices.

Below are two "shopbot" sites based in the UK and in France.

This is a search for an Asterix book, using a shopbot site.

Stores such as amazon.com and bol.com sell books, CDs, videos and more in countries around the world.

Selecting and paying

Most online stores have a virtual shopping basket or trolley or cart, and when you decide you would like to buy an item, you add it to the shopping basket. You can then go back and look around the store site some more, and maybe find other things you would like to buy. You can always change your mind and take an item out of the basket if you decide not to buy it.

When you have finished choosing, click on your shopping basket and proceed to the virtual checkout. Here you will give your contact and credit card details, and arrange for the goods to be sent to you by post or a delivery service.

Shopping Web sites

Find direct links to all these sites at **www.usborne-quicklinks.com**

Some of the most extensive Web sites for books, music, video, DVD and games are **Amazon**, **Barnes and Noble** (in the US), **bol.com** (in Europe and the Far East) and **MVC** (in the UK).

Sites for comparing prices include **ShopSmart** in the UK, **Kelkoo** in the UK and other European countries and **mySimon** in the US.

Is it safe to shop on the Internet?

Many people are concerned about shopping on the Internet. How can you be sure you are dealing with a reliable company? Is it safe to give your credit card details over the Internet? What happens if something goes wrong, and you don't get the goods you ordered?

Know who you are buying from As with any kind of shopping, you can take some precautions. Try to deal with established businesses – companies which also have stores on the high street, or well-known Internet companies that have been trading for a few years.

Many shopping sites have a page entitled "About us", or similar, telling you more about the company. You can also look for a "Contact us" page, where you can find e-mail addresses and telephone numbers in case you have any questions about your order.

Be careful when giving personal details Sometimes Web sites will offer you special discounts or gifts to encourage you to visit them again, and will ask for your name and address. You should only give your personal details to well-known, well-established companies.

Use a secure server Some people don't think it is a good idea to give your credit card details on the Internet. It might be possible for criminals to intercept a Web page, take your details and steal money from your account.

In practice, this is rare, especially as most Internet companies use a process called "encryption" to keep your card details safe. When you send your details, they are translated using a special code, so that only the company server can decode them, and the code is different for every transaction.

Some Web sites have a page explaining this process. Otherwise, look for a message telling you that you are about to send information over a "secure server", and a closed padlock symbol at the bottom of your browser window.

Get confirmation of your order Usually companies will send you e-mail confirmation of your order, and the e-mail may tell you what to do if you don't receive what you asked for. Otherwise, make a note of the details on the "Contact us" page, as mentioned above, so that you can call the company if you need to.

Food, gifts and travel

Shopping on the Internet can make your life easier in many ways. You can use the Internet to order groceries or take-away meals. You can find imaginative presents for special occasions, and have them delivered. Specialist travel sites help you plan a holiday and compare prices, right up to the last minute. You can find direct links to all the sites on these pages at **www.usborne-quicklinks.com**

Meals online

You can use the Internet to find recipes and even buy the ingredients. Many grocery stores have Web sites where you can search for recipe ideas and find out about different kinds of food. You can order groceries online, and arrange for them to be delivered to your home.

If you don't feel like cooking, you could use a restaurant directory site to find a restaurant in your area. You place your order online, and then choose whether to collect your meal from the restaurant or have it delivered to you.

This is one UK supermarket which can deliver groceries ordered over the Internet.

You can order take-away meals from this site in the US.

Something special

There are lots of sites where you can find great ideas for presents – chocolate and other fine foods from around the world, flowers, jewellery, gifts for the home and more. On some sites you can choose from a list of occasions (birthday, Mother's Day and so on) and types of present, and you will get a list of suggestions for gift ideas. You can even type in the date of someone's birthday, and you will be sent a reminder by e-mail in time for you to choose a present for them.

When you choose a bouquet or a present online, it can be gift-wrapped and delivered with your personal message. The Spanish Web site shown below specializes in gifts and flowers.

Web sites for food and gifts

Find direct links to all these sites at **www.usborne-quicklinks.com**

Find food facts, cooking tips and delicacies to buy online, as well as over 12,000 recipes at the US's **Epicurious** Web site. (The site uses US measures: find conversions to UK metric and imperial measures, as well as recipes from celebrity chefs, at **The Food Web**)

Choose flowers, chocolates or other gifts at **allpresent.com** – if you can't afford the real thing, send "virtual flowers" via e-mail.

Holidays and travel

Online travel agencies are very popular and offer lots of help in arranging travel and holidays. Many rail networks and airlines allow you to book tickets online as well as check timetables at their Web sites (see page 61).

If you are looking for airline tickets, there are several online travel agencies which will search for the best fare for you. Type in your journey details and dates and times, and you will get a short list of the best fares available.

Besides travel agencies, you'll find a huge amount of useful information and advice, so that you can be truly well-prepared for your journey.

With the Internet, it's never too late to plan a trip or an evening out, or choose a present for someone...

Many online travel agencies offer not only ticket deals but also maps, destination guides, special reports and travel tips – even online phrasebooks.

The site on the left specializes in shopping around for the best flight prices.

The site below is not a travel agency, but a fantastic guide to destinations around the world, with information on everything from attractions and special events to the weather.

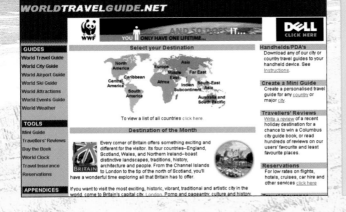

Travel Web sites

Find direct links to all these sites at **www.usborne-quicklinks.com**

One of the most popular online travel agents is **Expedia**, offering a range of travel services and tips. **Travelocity** has a useful fare search service.

For information on destinations, look at the **World Travel Guide**, or the Web sites of leading travel publishers **Rough Guides** and **Lonely Planet**.

For practical advice on visas, health and safe travel, check the UK **Foreign Office Travel Advice** Web site or the US **Department of State Consular Information Sheets**.

Health and money matters

The Internet can help you manage your life in all kinds of ways. You will find health advice, online banks, investment advice and virtual money. You can also use the Internet to contribute to charities worldwide. You can find direct links to all the sites on these pages at **www.usborne-quicklinks.com**

Good health

Healthcare organizations publish a mass of useful information online, both to help you lead a healthier life and to tell you more about particular health problems and how to deal with them.

Always remember that a Web site is no substitute for a real doctor, and if you are concerned, you should take proper medical advice. However, a well-established healthcare site can give you a huge amount of background information, reassurance and sensible advice.

The UK's NetDoctor Web site offers a vast amount of reliable, readable information on health matters.

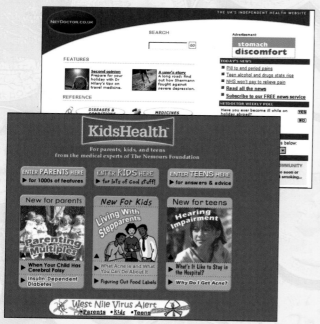

The KidsHealth site is actually three sites in one, with hundreds of excellent articles on health concerns for kids, teens and parents.

Managing your money

Internet banking can be a very convenient way to manage your finances. You can see your account details 24 hours a day, and arrange to pay bills or take out a loan online in minutes. Online banks use advanced encryption techniques to keep your account details safe (see page 67 for more about encryption).

If you are interested in investing money, you will find lots of information and advice on the Internet, from beginners' guides to highly specialized information. Many well-regarded financial institutions offer useful information on their Web sites, completely free of charge.

Remember that you have to be over 18 to open a current account, to pay by credit card or to buy and sell on the Internet.

Patagon is an online bank for Spanish and Latin American clients.

TheStreet.com offers up-to-the-minute financial news, while The Motley Fool®has an excellent beginners' guide to investing.

Virtual money

Most sites which accept payment on the Internet rely on credit cards, but there are other ways of paying for goods online. The Mondex payment system, which is highly secure, is supported by banks around the world. You can transfer money from a bank account to a Mondex smart card, and then pay for goods online using your smart card. Unlike credit cards, you do not have to be over 18 years old to have a Mondex account.

Mondex' smart card system makes it possible to pay for goods securely online.

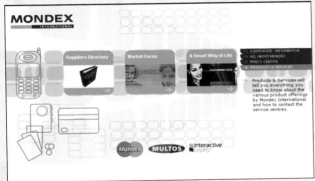

The French medical aid organisation Médecins Sans Frontières has an online scheme to donate meals to Third World countries.

Money, health and charity Web sites

Find direct links to all these sites at **www.usborne-quicklinks.com**

Find masses of healthcare information on the **KidsHealth** Web site. **NetDoctor** and **NHSDirect** offer health advice for the UK.

Online banks include **Egg** and **Smile** in the UK, and **citi.com** in the US. You can find financial advice at **Bloomberg**, **ft.com**, **TheStreet.com**, **FTMarketWatch** and **The Motley Fool**.

Find out more about virtual money on the **Mondex** Web site.

Well-known charities online include **Save the Children**, **Unicef** and **The Hunger Site**.

Helping others

You can find out about charitable organizations around the world on the Internet. Charity Web sites can tell you how and where the charities work, and keep you up to date with their news. You can also make donations online.

Save the Children's Web site: you can have fun helping charity, too.

Sports online

The Internet is a great place for keeping up to date with sports results, finding in-depth coverage of matches and reading your team's news on their Web site. You can also find out about unusual sports, plan sporting holidays and buy equipment.

You can find direct links to all the sites on these pages at **www.usborne-quicklinks.com**

Sports news

The main television news networks (see page 59) have excellent sports coverage on their Web sites, including the latest results at the time you connect to their site. Many sites' sports pages will update results automatically while you are looking at the page; with others, you can click on the *Refresh* button at the top of your browser window to update the page.

This is CNN/Sports Illustrated's home page.

Teamtalk is a UK-based site specializing in breaking sports news.

These are the official team sites of Barcelona, Olympique de Marseille and Juventus football clubs.

League and team sites

You will find official Web sites for all the most popular sports and sporting events. If you don't know a site's URL, you will find lists of links to hundreds of sports sites in a directory such as Yahoo!® (see page 48). Yahoo! lists links for around a hundred different kinds of sport, from archery to windsurfing.

Sports.com has pages dedicated to different sports in five languages.

The Web site of the German premier soccer league

Webcams

Web cameras, or Webcams, are like television cameras connected to the Internet. You can buy a small version to attach to your computer and use at home. You could use a Webcam to record video clips to include in a Web site, for example, or attach to e-mails. You can also visit Web sites to look at the views from Webcams around the world. Usually the images broadcast on the Web are not actually moving, but are updated every few minutes.

Winter sports

If you are a skier or a snowboarder, you will find lots of good sites with information about the sport itself, resorts and equipment. You can find holiday offers and weather reports, as well as news and tips on technique. There are even pages where you can read other people's equipment reviews, or post your own.

On some winter sports sites there are links to "snowcams" – Webcams in ski resorts worldwide – so that you can check out the snow before you head for the slopes.

Click to view full-size image
06-18-01 08:48 AM
BLue Sky and Lots of Snow. Don't forget your sunscreen.

This site has lots of useful information for skiers. Linked sites cater for golf, diving and snowboarding.

Sports Web sites

Find direct links to all these sites at **www.usborne-quicklinks.com**

For up-to-the-minute sports news, try **CNN-Sports Illustrated**, **BBC Online Sport**, **Teamtalk**, **Sportal** or **sports.com**

Top European soccer teams have some great Web sites, with news, game reviews, picture galleries, playing tips and fun downloads. Find links to seven of the best at the foot of **Sportal**'s opening page.

Useful sites for winter sports include **SkiCentral**, which has links to snowcams around the world, and **ifyouski.com**.

Games

If you are interested in playing games on your computer, you'll find links to all kinds on the Internet, from traditional board games to the latest 3-D action spectaculars. You can download games onto your computer and play by yourself, or you can join in online with other players around the world.

You can find direct links to all the sites on these pages at **www.usborne-quicklinks.com**

Finding games online

Games on the Internet are "hosted" on computers called servers. To play, you need to find a link to the server which is hosting the game you want. You'll find a list of links on a portal such as Yahoo!® or MSN®. If you know the name of the game you want, you could try using a search engine such as Google℠.

Many games sites will ask you to register before you play. Read any information that they give you carefully before supplying your details. Make sure you can easily find contact details on the site, and that you can tick a box if you don't want to be contacted by e-mail, otherwise you may be sent unwanted "spam" (see page 28).

Below you can see part of the tutorial session for a game called Alchemy, at the MSN Gaming Zone

What hardware do I need?

If you are playing simple card or board games via the Internet, you don't need a powerful computer or extra hardware. However, to play 3-D action games online, you will need a high-speed Internet connection (preferably ISDN, cable or ADSL), a fast processor with plenty of RAM (300MHz with 64MB of RAM), a 4GB hard disk and a 3-D video acceleration card. If you are going to play games a lot, you may also want to buy some gaming accessories, such as joysticks, gamepads or steering wheels.

This arcade-style snowboard challenge is one of the many games available on the Bonus.com Web site.

Do I need extra software?

To play a game on the Internet, you sometimes need client software. This is a program that allows your computer to communicate with the server hosting the game. For example, to play chess, you will need a chess client.

Most games sites on the Internet include links for you to download all the software you need to play a game. Some sites, such as the Yahoo!® chess site, will prompt you to install the software: all you need to do is to click *Yes*. A lot of the software available is free, but you may have to pay for some of it. You can find out more about downloading software from the Internet on pages 46-47.

Multi-user gaming

One of the amazing things about the Internet is that you can play games against people in other parts of the world when you're online. You'll find these games, known as multi-user games, on most games sites. You can even play action games against other users if you have a fast computer that can process the data quickly (see below). Some CD-ROM games have a multi-user facility which allows you to play with other online users who have the same game.

Ping and lag

Speed is all-important in online action games. You need to have quick reactions yourself, but you also need your computer to signal your actions quickly to the game server. The time this takes is known as "ping", and it will be much faster if you have a high-speed Internet connection.

　　If your ping isn't very fast, there will be a time-lag, or "lag", before your actions appear on screen. Lag is particularly noticeable with gamers playing in countries that are far apart. You can improve lag by looking for game servers in countries close to you.

Console games

Some games consoles now have built-in modems and the capacity to link to the Internet. Users of game machines such as the Sega® Dreamcast® can connect to the Internet and play online. The new Microsoft® Xbox console has a built-in port for high-speed Internet connection.

Avoid the hazards, win the race, destroy the monster, save the planet...

Only a game...

Once you've started playing, it's easy to get involved, and hard to stop when you're sure you can better your score with just one more game. Don't forget, though: too much time online is bad for your eyesight and your general health, and if you are paying for your time online, it can become very expensive. Don't let the game take over – keep games sessions short.

The Xbox is designed to adapt to online multi-user gaming.

Games on the Internet

Find direct links to all these sites at **www.usborne-quicklinks.com**

Good places to start looking for games include **Yahoo!® Games** and the **MSN Gaming Zone**. Kids' site **Bonus.com** also has a great selection of games and puzzles.

Find all kinds of games, from board games to CD-ROM classics, at **Flipside UK**.

Find news and reviews of PC and console games on the **Gamespot** Web site.

Find more about the Xbox console and games on the **Xbox** Web site.

Web-based e-mail

Most people have e-mail addresses at their school, college or place of work, or at home through their ISP (see pages 12-13). However, many people find it useful to have a Web-based e-mail account, or Webmail account, as well or instead. A Webmail account allows you to send and receive e-mail from any computer with a browser and Internet connection, anywhere in the world. This is useful if you travel a lot, or if you don't have your own computer. These two pages show you how to set up a Web-based account.

How does it work?

With normal e-mail, your messages are stored on a computer run by a service provider. Your ISP links your e-mail account with your computer, so it will always send your mail on to the same place.

Web-based e-mail is also stored on a service provider's computer, but it can be accessed by any browser on any computer, using a unique access name and password.

Choosing a service

You will see a list of popular Webmail providers in the box on the page opposite. They provide a free service, which means that you pay nothing for using the service itself (although you pay as usual for time you spend online). However, you will probably see advertisements on your e-mails when you use free providers, as this is how they make their money.

Signing up

To open a Web-based e-mail account, you need to sign up on the registration page of a Webmail provider, such as those listed in the box opposite. Go to the registration page, then follow the easy instructions you are given.

Filling in a form

When you sign up, most providers will ask you to fill in an online form similar to the one below.

YAHOO! Mail

Help - Yahoo!

Sign up for your Yahoo! ID with Mail   Already have an ID? Sign In

Get a Yahoo! ID and password for access to Yahoo! Mail and all other personalized Yahoo! services.

Yahoo! ID: [＿＿＿＿＿] @ yahoo.com
(examples: "lildude56" or "goody2shoes")

Password: [＿＿＿＿＿]

Re-type Password: [＿＿＿＿＿]

Choosing your ID
You will use this information to access Yahoo! each time. Capitalization matters for your password!

If you forget your password, we would identify you with this information.

Security Question: [[select a question to answer] ▼]

Your Answer: [＿＿＿＿＿]

Birthday: [[select one] ▼] [＿] , [＿] (Month Day, Year)

Current Email (Optional): [＿＿＿＿＿]

Recalling your password
This is our only way to verify your identity. To protect your account, make sure "your answer" is memorable for you but hard for others to guess!

This is part of the form that you fill out to sign up for the Yahoo! Mail service.

You'll be asked to choose an ID or username and a password. The password will allow you to open the mailbox where your messages are stored, and will prevent other people from reading your messages. Use a password you'll remember easily (find password advice on page 16).

If you do forget your password, some providers, such as Yahoo!®, will ask you a question – the date of your birthday, for example, or your pet's name – so you may be asked to give this information on the sign-up form. Others, like Excite℠, will ask you to enter a phrase that will remind you of your password.

Um, er, what was my password, again?

excite Sign Up

1. **2.** 3. simple steps gets you FREE...

Mail + Chat + My Excite Start Page + Portfolio

1. Choose Your Login Information - 6-20 characters, only letters, numbers, and dashes

Member Name: [＿＿]

Password: [＿＿]

Re-enter Password: [＿＿]

Inside the US? Click here.

2. Password Reminder Phrase - In case you forget your password
Enter a phrase that will remind you of your password. For example, if your password is the name of the town where you were born, you might enter "the town where I was born".

Hint Phrase: [＿＿]

3. Personalization Information - Information to provide customized features
Get local weather reports and events, your horoscope, and other cool features
(At Excite we value your privacy and guarantee to adhere to the policies of TRUSTe)

Given Name: [＿＿]

This form asks you to suggest a phrase or question, in case you forget your password.

Using Web-based e-mail

To use your Web-based e-mail service, open up your browser and type in the mail service's URL. Enter your access name and password and your personal page will appear.

A personal page from the Yahoo! Mail service

You can use the service to send and receive messages. Most services offer a spell checker and an address book, and some let you send attachments, generally under 1MB in size. However, you may find messages take longer to arrive or longer to download than those sent using an ordinary e-mail account, and the service provider's advertising can be distracting.

Picking up messages

You can use any online computer to access your messages wherever you are in the world. There are more and more Internet cafés around the world, which makes it easier to access Web-based e-mail accounts. Libraries, colleges and large stores are other places to try.

You can send and receive e-mail from an Internet café, like this one in Paris.

 ## Spam and viruses

Web-based e-mail, like any other kind, is at risk from viruses – although large organizations such as Hotmail will take care to protect themselves against virus infections. As always, if you receive an e-mail from an address you don't recognize, the best thing to do is to delete it without opening it.

If you receive advertising mailings that you don't want (known as "spam", see page 28), see if there is an "unsubscribe" option in the e-mail itself. If you continue to receive unwanted messages, look for a filter option such as Hotmail's "Block Sender". This stops any more e-mail from the same source before it reaches your Inbox.

If you ever receive offensive messages, don't respond to them, even if you are invited to unsubscribe – just delete them and block the sender's address.

Web-based e-mail services

Below are some of the most popular free e-mail providers on the Internet. You can find direct links to them all at **www.usborne-quicklinks.com**

MSN® Hotmail® operates worldwide, and has millions of members – the drawback to this is that it may be hard to choose a username that hasn't already been allocated.

Yahoo!® also operates worldwide, but has local sites for over twenty countries. Other popular providers include **AltaVista®**, **Excite^SM**, **Lycos®** and **Netscape®**.

Messenger services and chat

You can use the messenger services offered by AOL (see page 14), MSN® or Yahoo!® to contact your friends instantly online. You type a conversation and – unlike e-mail – what you and your friends type appears almost at once in your browser window. You can also find Web-based chat rooms which work in a similar way, except that they are open to more people.

You can find direct links to all the sites on these pages at **www.usborne-quicklinks.com**

Messenger services

To use a messenger service, first you need to download some software from the Web site that runs the service. Go to the messenger service page of the site and you will find full instructions there. If you already have an account with the service provider, you can use your existing screen name, ID or username, otherwise you will need to choose one.

Once you have installed the software, add your friends to your Friend or Contact or Buddy list. They will need either to have an account with the same service provider or to sign up to the messenger service themselves. Once this is done, you can send them instant messages and chat to them when they are online.

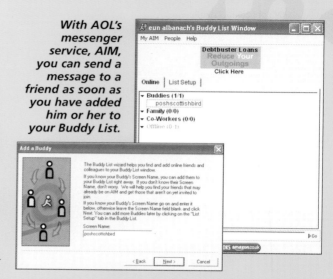

With AOL's messenger service, AIM, you can send a message to a friend as soon as you have added him or her to your Buddy List.

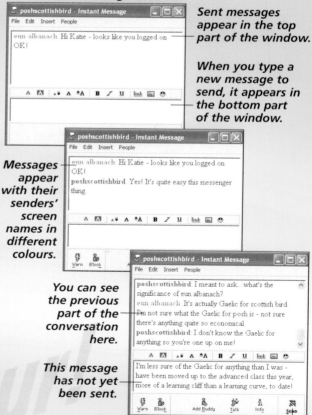

This is AIM's message window.

Sent messages appear in the top part of the window.

When you type a new message to send, it appears in the bottom part of the window.

Messages appear with their senders' screen names in different colours.

You can see the previous part of the conversation here.

This message has not yet been sent.

Click on this button to send your message, or press the return key.

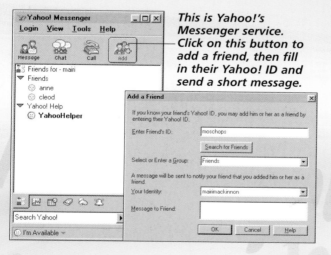

This is Yahoo!'s Messenger service. Click on this button to add a friend, then fill in their Yahoo! ID and send a short message.

Chat rooms

There are huge numbers of "chat rooms" on the Internet, where people can log in and chat about any subject under the sun. As with messenger services, you type a conversation, but since chat rooms are open to anyone who can log in, there can be many more people taking part at any one time.

If you use an online service such as AOL (see page 14), you will find that it has a number of chat rooms for its members only, both general and specialized in subjects such as music or sport or for kids and teens. Otherwise you can sign up to join a chat room on the Internet.

Signing up

You will have to register before you can join in a chat session. This involves choosing a username, and giving your age and e-mail address or parents' e-mail address if you are registering for a kids' or teens' chat room.

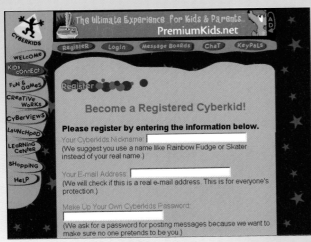

This is part of the registration form for the Cyberkids Web site.

Once your registration has been accepted, you can log in to the chat sessions. You may like to see how the session is going for a while before you join in. This is known as "lurking", and helps you to get a feel for the chat style. Join in when you feel ready, and have fun!

Safe chatting

Be careful when using online chat. Although it can be sociable and fun, some people may write offensive and unpleasant things. Remember, too, that people online may not be exactly who they say they are. If you can't see someone or hear their voice, you have no idea whether they are male or female, eight years old or 80.

If you visit online chat rooms, it's best to find ones which are monitored (supervised). Some chat rooms use monitoring software which blocks offensive words, but people can find ways around the block, so look for chat rooms monitored by real people.

Never give out personal information, such as your real name, address, telephone number or e-mail address, to someone you meet in a chat room. Never agree to meet up in real life – keep online friendships online.

If you read things you find offensive on a monitored site, the site monitor should stop the person concerned and may prevent them from accessing the site again. If you find offensive material on an unmonitored site, you can still report it to the site's managers – there is usually an e-mail link which you can use to contact them. They can then take steps to stop whoever is sending out the material.

Messenger services and chat sites

Find direct links to all these sites at **www.usborne-quicklinks.com**

Messenger services include **AOL Instant Messenger^SM(AIM)**, **Microsoft® Messenger** and **Yahoo® Messenger**.

Monitored chat rooms for kids and teens include the **Headbone Zone** and **KidsCom**. These are based in the US, so are generally open only in the evenings UK time.

The **BBC** Web site also offers monitored chat sessions, often with celebrity guests.

Creating your own Web site

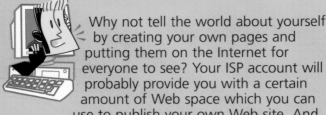

Why not tell the world about yourself by creating your own pages and putting them on the Internet for everyone to see? Your ISP account will probably provide you with a certain amount of Web space which you can use to publish your own Web site. And it's easy to obtain the software you need to create your pages.

Why build your own Web site?

A Web site is a great way of communicating with people. You might like to build a site for your family and friends, with news and photos. You might share a passion for a subject, such as pets or music or a place you know well. If you have a business, you may want to advertise your products or services.

You will see amazing sites on the Web with fantastic pictures, animations, sound clips and games. People can spend vast amounts of time and money on making their site look good. But you don't need to be a Web expert to produce a good basic site. This part of the book shows you that it's easy to build a well-designed site of your own.

Below you can see some personal home pages from around the world. You can find links to them at www.usborne-quicklinks.com

Does design really matter?

There are billions of sites on the Web, and more are being added every day. There are no "design police" on the Web, in fact anyone can publish anything as long as it is legal. However, if you want people to enjoy visiting your site, you should try to make it as attractive and easy to use as you can. This part of the book is full of tips to help you to do that.

What hardware do I need?

You can use either a PC or a Macintosh computer to create a Web site. You don't need a brand-new or very powerful computer to build a basic Web site, but do make sure you can connect to the Internet easily.

Most Web site design software is designed for Microsoft® Windows® 95 or later versions of Windows, or Macintosh OS8.5 or later versions, so make sure you have one of these as your computer's operating system.

It's a good idea to look at quite a few Web sites to give you ideas before you start. Make sure you don't have to spend too long downloading them. It helps to have a fast modem, preferably 56K. There are faster connections available, such as ISDN or ADSL, but they tend to be expensive for home use.

Josep Fornell uses his home page to tell people about his rally driving team in Catalonia, Spain.

The Reinhardt family's page design is simple and elegant.

11-year-old Craig Williams created his own art gallery online.

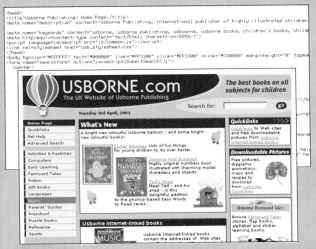

Dreamweaver is a Web editor often used by professional designers.

This is the Usborne Web site as it appears on screen, and above it the HTML code for the beginning of the home page.

Web design software

You can build a Web site in various ways. All Web sites are built up with a programming language called HTML (HyperText Mark-up Language). You can see what this looks like by using your browser to visit a Web site, then clicking on *View* and then *Source* (or *Page Source*) in your browser's toolbar. If you have never seen HTML before, it looks like gibberish, but in fact you don't really need to learn it to create a site.

If you have Microsoft® Word on your computer, you can use Word to create a fairly basic Web page, in much the same way that you create a document for printing out. However, if you want to create a more sophisticated-looking page, you will want to use a Web editor.

Benjamin Camara has created an impressive Web site in French and English.

What is a Web editor?

A Web editor is a program which produces HTML but shows you on screen what the Web page will look like. This is known as WYSIWYG (What You See Is What You Get).

There are a number of popular Web editors to choose from. Microsoft® FrontPage®, the Web editor used in this book, is available in some countries as an inexpensive or free trial version for 30-45 days. After that, you can pay for the full version if you want to keep it. Netscape® Composer is a Web editor included free with the Netscape® package.

When you have tried designing a Web page with a basic Web editor, you might like to look at one with more features. For example, Macromedia® Dreamweaver® is a Web editor which is popular with Web design professionals. It, too, is available as a free trial version.

You can obtain many of these editors via the Internet – there are links to some useful Web sites on the Usborne Quicklinks Web site at **www.usborne-quicklinks.com**

A picture gallery page created by the Thiboutot family, in Canada

Planning your Web site

A Web editor makes it easy to start creating a Web site right away. Even so, it's worth spending a little time planning your site first, and collecting the material you want to use – text, pictures and so on.

Surfing for inspiration

The best place to get ideas for your Web site is on the Web itself. Look at a variety of Web sites, and decide which design ideas you like and which you think don't work so well. You may not have the same resources as the designers who created the sites, but you can still judge whether a site uses colours nicely or looks cluttered and complicated.

If you are not sure where to start looking, try some of the sites featured in this book. Many of these sites not only have useful content but are also well-designed.

When you find a site you like, make sure that you can come back to it at a later date by bookmarking it or adding it to your Favorites (see page 42).

Collecting material

You can include all sorts of things on your Web site. The most common to start with are text and pictures, but you may want to add sound, video or animations as well. You can also have links to other sites you particularly like. Don't worry if you don't have all your material ready right away. You can always add more pages to your site later.

It's a good idea to have a special folder on your computer for all the things you plan to put on your site. This makes it easy to find and place pictures or other elements when you are designing your site. When you come to upload your site (publish it on the Internet), you will need to send a lot of this material to the ISP or other organization which is hosting it, too.

The best place to create this folder is in the My Documents folder, which you can see on your computer's desktop on the left-hand side of the screen. When you are saving files for your Web site, make sure each file has a different name. It's best to make filenames no more than eight characters long.

Copyright

While you are surfing other people's sites, you may see some great pictures and animations. Don't be tempted to copy these for use on your own site, however. Pictures and information on the Internet may be available for anyone to look at and read, but they are still generally in copyright (see page 43).

Some pictures are "copyright-free", which means they are available for anyone to use. You can find out more about this on page 88. If you want to use any other pictures or text you have found, you must get permission from the person or company that owns the copyright. If you don't do this, you may be breaking the law.

Thumbnail sketches help you to plan your site.

Mapping out your site

When you have decided what you want to include on your Web site, you may find that you have enough material for several pages or more. Think about how you will organize the site. You will need to create a "home page" – an introductory page that tells visitors what information your site contains, and that has links to other pages on the site.

Divide your material between pages. Don't be tempted to put too much on one page. It's much more effective to share the content between several shorter pages instead.

It's a good idea to group different kinds of information. For example, lots of Web sites include a picture gallery, with a collection of pictures or photos on one page. (You can find out more about picture galleries on page 97.) If you are including links to other sites, you can keep them all together on a "links" page.

This is a fairly typical home page.

The Mackinnon Family Home Page

about us
picture gallery
the Isle of Skye
the band
cool links
contact us

Standing on the doorstep at a friend's house last summer. My brother is not actually 6½ft tall and I don't usually wear a tiara around the house. The picture was taken on the morning of my wedding

These are links to other pages on the site.

Designing page layout

Try sketching the pages of your site on paper. Quick sketches called "thumbnails", like the ones shown above, can help you decide where to put text and pictures. Think about a general theme or mood for your site, and how you might create this – by using similar colours, for example, or similar designs on different pages.

There are a few things to remember when you are planning page layout. People download Web sites to different computers, and different screen sizes may not show your whole page width. Put important information, such as the page title, where it can easily be seen (towards the top of the page, on the left or in the centre). Don't put links on the right of the page where they may be overlooked. If you are using text, don't make the text area too wide.

Above all, avoid putting too many pictures, animations or other "extras" on your home page. This will make the page take a long time to download, which is frustrating for visitors to your site.

⚠ Be safe

Millions of Internet users will be able to see the information on your Web site. If you are creating a personal site, don't include anything private, such as your home address or telephone number.

Your first Web page

Once you are ready to start creating Web pages, find and open your Web editor. The Web editor used in this book is Microsoft® FrontPage®.

If you have Microsoft® Office installed on your computer, it may already include a copy of FrontPage. Click on the Start button at the bottom left-hand corner of your screen, then on Programs, and look for Microsoft FrontPage in the list that comes up. Click on it to open the program.

If you don't have FrontPage already installed, you may be able to order a trial copy from Microsoft. Go to **www.usborne-quicklinks.com** to find out more.

Introducing FrontPage

If you are familiar with Microsoft® Word, you will find that FrontPage looks similar and many tools and commands are the same. As in Word, if you let your cursor rest over a button or symbol, a label will appear telling you what it is.

When you open FrontPage, you will see an empty window like the one shown below.*

The opening window looks like this.

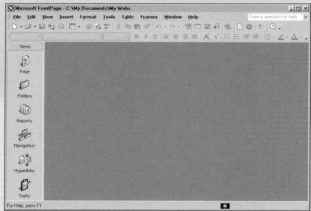

Click on *File* in the top left-hand corner of the screen, then on *New* and then *Page or Web...* in the drop-down menus that appear. Select **Empty Web** and then **One Page Web** from the options given, and click *OK*. Then click on the blank paper icon at the top left-hand corner of the screen.

A basic home page

Try creating a basic home page using FrontPage. Your page will need a title, and you may also like to include a little information about yourself. You can add a picture or other decoration later, if you like.

Double-click on the icon entitled index.htm in the Folder List on the left of the FrontPage window. In the page area on the right, type your page title and a short introductory piece, as on the page below.

The folder list shows you all the files and folders that make up your Web site. You can close and open it by clicking this button.

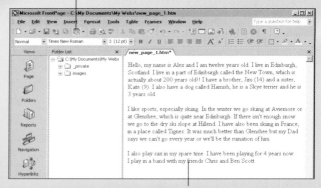

This is how your page might look.

Now you can try formatting the text a little. Select a piece of text by highlighting it with your mouse. You can then make it bold, centre it or change the size.

Click here to change the size of your highlighted text, and select a text size. — *Click here for bold.*

Click here to centre your highlighted text.

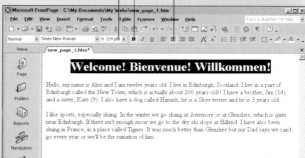

*FrontPage 2000 and earlier versions open

Saving your Web page

As with any work you do on your computer, you should save your Web page often. When you do, FrontPage automatically creates a special folder called My Webs so that you can find your page and open it again easily another time.

Saving your page

To save your page, click on *File* in the Menu bar at the top of the screen, and click on *Save* in the drop-down menu that appears.

Click here.

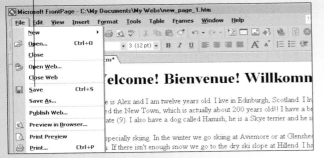

The first time you do this, a Save As window will appear, like the one below. Your page will be saved as index.htm, which indicates that it is your site's home page. The page title (which will appear at the top of the browser window when the page is published) is given as Home Page, but you can change it if you like by clicking on *Change...* Then click on *Save*.

When you click on *Save* again, your page will automatically be saved with the same settings.

The Save As window

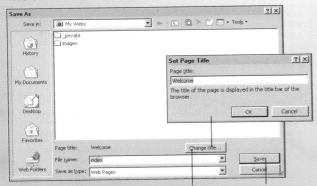

Click here to change the page title.   **Click here to save the page.**

Closing and reopening your page

FrontPage saves your page in a folder called My Webs, which is in the My Documents folder. You can now close down FrontPage, but you will still be able to go back to your page and open it again.

When you reopen FrontPage, click on *File* and then on *Open...* in the drop-down menu that appears. Alternatively, click on the opening folder icon in the toolbar below the menu bar.

Click here.

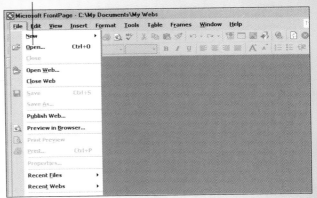

FrontPage will show you all the files in My Webs, including your saved page. Click on *Open...* or double-click on the filename to open the page.

Here is your saved page.

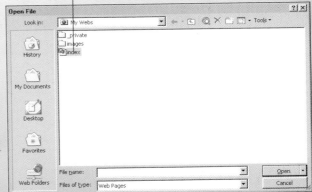

Changing text

You can vary the appearance of text on a Web page to make it easier to read. By dividing up blocks of text, and choosing the right typeface, you can make your page look better and more attractive altogether.

Breaking up blocks of text

Text is generally harder to read on screen than it is on the page of a book, so think how to make it easier for visitors to your site. Large blocks of text are difficult and tiring to read, so use lots of short paragraphs rather than a few long ones.

When you finish a paragraph, press the Return key. Microsoft® FrontPage® will automatically insert a line space before the next paragraph. You can see this in the first page below.

(If for any reason you *don't* want a line space, hold down the Shift key and then press the Return key.)

This page is much easier to read...

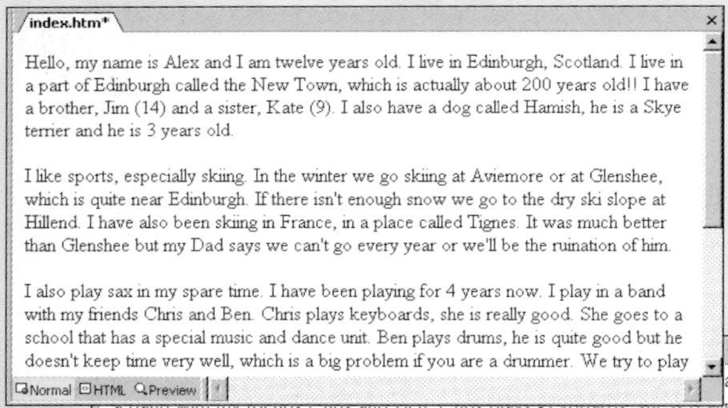

> **index.htm***
>
> Hello, my name is Alex and I am twelve years old. I live in Edinburgh, Scotland. I live in a part of Edinburgh called the New Town, which is actually about 200 years old!! I have a brother, Jim (14) and a sister, Kate (9). I also have a dog called Hamish, he is a Skye terrier and he is 3 years old.
>
> I like sports, especially skiing. In the winter we go skiing at Aviemore or at Glenshee, which is quite near Edinburgh. If there isn't enough snow we go to the dry ski slope at Hillend. I have also been skiing in France, in a place called Tignes. It was much better than Glenshee but my Dad says we can't go every year or we'll be the ruination of him.
>
> I also play sax in my spare time. I have been playing for 4 years now. I play in a band with my friends Chris and Ben. Chris plays keyboards, she is really good. She goes to a school that has a special music and dance unit. Ben plays drums, he is quite good but he doesn't keep time very well, which is a big problem if you are a drummer. We try to play
>
> Normal HTML Preview

> a band with my friends Chris and Ben. Chris plays keyboards, she is really good. She goes to a school that has a special music and dance unit. Ben plays drums, he is quite good but he doesn't keep time very well, which is a big problem if you are a drummer. We try to play every weekend but it doesn't always work out, especially if Ben is playing rugby, he is in the junior team at his school so he quite often has a game. Another friend, Sam, used to play bass but he went to live in England so we are looking for a bass player at the moment. Last summer we all went on music camp in Aberdeen. We had a brilliant time and met some other really good bands. I like listening to famous sax players like Stan Getz. I wish I could play like that, though my teacher says it's OK if you're Stan Getz but mere mortals like you and I have to play by the book and don't you forget it young Alex. My teacher is excellent, he is always making me laugh, he always pretends to be grumpy but he isn't really.
>
> Normal HTML Preview

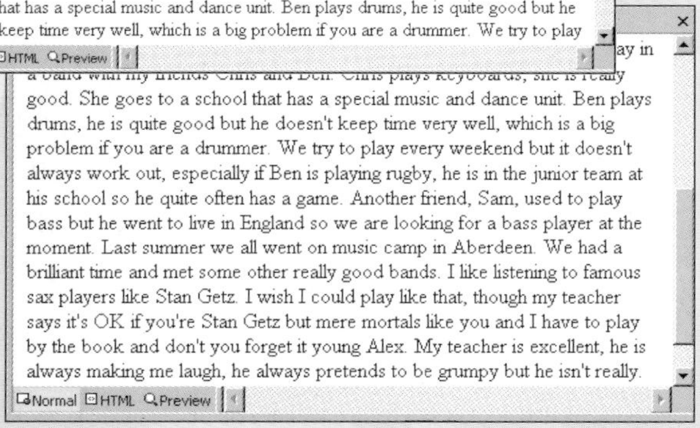

...than this one.

Different sizes and styles

On page 84, you saw how to increase type size, and make type bold. These are good ways of making a piece of text stand out, for example as a page title or a heading.

There are seven sizes of type you can use on a Web page. They are shown below.

These are the various type sizes you can use for text.

This is size one

This is size two

This is size three

This is size four

This is size five

This is size six

and size seven

You can also use bold, italic and underlined type. However, bear in mind that italic type can be hard to read on screen, and underlining is generally used for hyperlinks, so to save confusion, avoid using it for other purposes.

Using different type sizes, and maybe bold type for titles and headings, can make a Web page look more interesting and readable.

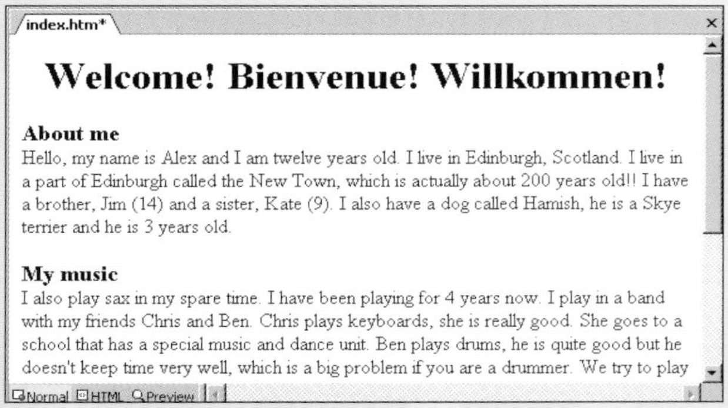

> **index.htm***
>
> ### Welcome! Bienvenue! Willkommen!
>
> **About me**
> Hello, my name is Alex and I am twelve years old. I live in Edinburgh, Scotland. I live in a part of Edinburgh called the New Town, which is actually about 200 years old!! I have a brother, Jim (14) and a sister, Kate (9). I also have a dog called Hamish, he is a Skye terrier and he is 3 years old.
>
> **My music**
> I also play sax in my spare time. I have been playing for 4 years now. I play in a band with my friends Chris and Ben. Chris plays keyboards, she is really good. She goes to a school that has a special music and dance unit. Ben plays drums, he is quite good but he doesn't keep time very well, which is a big problem if you are a drummer. We try to play
>
> Normal HTML Preview

The section headings on the page above are a size bigger than the main text, and are in bold type.

Changing the font

You can make a piece of text more readable by changing the typeface, or font. You may have quite a few fonts installed on your own computer, but other computers will only display text using the fonts they have, so it's best not to use anything too individual and unusual.

There are three main kinds of fonts:

Display fonts These are very decorative, and are good for making headings or key words stand out on paper, but not all computers have the same ones, so they are not ideal for Web pages. Some examples of display fonts are:

> **COPPERPLATE GOTHIC**
> *Brush Script*
> MATISSE

Serif fonts These are probably the most often-used fonts you will find in books and newspapers. "Serifs" are the little points on the ends of the letters. Some examples of serif fonts are:

> **Garamond**
> Palatino   Times

Sans serif fonts These fonts, without serifs, have a more modern feel. They are also generally easier to read on a computer screen. Some examples of sans serif fonts are:

> Arial
> Helvetica   Verdana

Verdana is a font developed especially for using in Web pages, as it is particularly easy to read on screen. If you have it on your computer, it might be a good one to use on your page.

To change the font in FrontPage, highlight a section of text and then click in the middle box in the formatting toolbar immediately above the page. Choose a font from the drop-down menu which appears.

Click here to select a font.

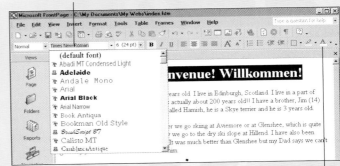

Click here to change the font colour.

Changing the font colour

You can also make text look more interesting by changing the colour. You do this by highlighting the text and clicking on the little black arrow beside the capital A in the formatting toolbar. This gives you a drop-down menu with a range of sixteen standard colours. You can click on *More Colors...* at the bottom of the menu for more choices.

You can have fun with different colours, but don't get carried away – too many colours will only be distracting.

This page, with dark blue text on a light blue background, using a sans serif font, is easy to read. The page below it is a mess!

Abair ach beagan agus abair gu math e • An rud a nithear gu math, chithear a bhuil • An uair a chluinneas tu sgeul gun dreach na creid i • Am fear a bhios fad aig an aiseig, gheibh e thairis uaireigin • A bheairt sin a bhios cearr, 'se foighidinn is fhear a dheanamh ris • An rud nach gabh leasachadh, 's feudar cur suas leis • Bu mhath an sgàthan sùil caraid • Beiridh caora dhubh uan as fhear an ùbhal is fhe...

Abair ach beagan agus abair gu math e • An rud a nithear gu math, chithear a bhuil • An uair a chluinneas tu sgeul gun dreach na creid i • Am fear a bhios fad aig an aiseig, gheibh e thairis uaireigin • A bheairt sin a bhios cearr, 'se foighidinn is fhear a dheanamh ris • An rud nach gabh leasachadh, 's feudar cur suas leis • Bu mhath an sgàthan sùil caraid • Beir an eigin air rudeigin a dheanamh

Putting pictures on your Web page

You can personalize your page and make it look more interesting by adding pictures. You can either use copyright-free pictures from the Internet, or prepare pictures of your own for placing on a Web page. These two pages tell you how to find and use ready-prepared pictures.

Clip art

Clip art is the name for pictures that you can use in personal documents. It is generally free of charge, and you don't have to ask permission from the artist or owner unless you are using the pictures for a commercial site. You should always credit the artist or owner, though (by giving their name underneath the picture).

Some clip art sites ask you to include a link back to their site. You can find out how to do this on page 93.

Where to find clip art

Microsoft® FrontPage® includes a selection of basic clip art pictures, but you will find many, many more on the Internet. You might start by looking on one of the sites listed below, or you could use a search engine (type in the search terms **free web clip art**).

Clip art Web sites

You'll find links to some useful clip art sites on the Usborne Quicklinks Web site, at **www.usborne-quicklinks.com**

For example, there are huge collections of images on the Web sites of **Clipart.com**, **Barry's Clipart Server** and **Clip Art Connection**. You'll also find some fun images at the **Clip Art Warehouse** Web site.

If you want to use photos on your site, there's a superb collection at **Freefoto.com**. Freefoto pictures are free to use on personal Web sites, but check the instructions for crediting them on the Usborne Quicklinks Web site.

Selecting and saving pictures

When you have found a picture that you like, save it from the Internet to your own computer by clicking on it with the right-hand button of your mouse. (If you are using a Macintosh computer, click and hold down your mouse button.) A menu will appear like the one below.

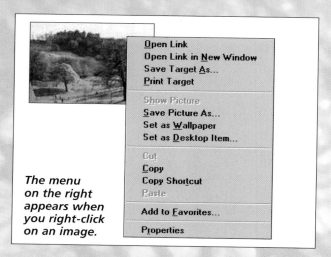

The menu on the right appears when you right-click on an image.

Click on *Save Picture As...* and a Save Picture window will appear, like the one below. Your browser will automatically give the picture a file name, and save it into the My Pictures folder in My Documents. You can change the file name if you want. Then click on *Save*.

The Save Picture window

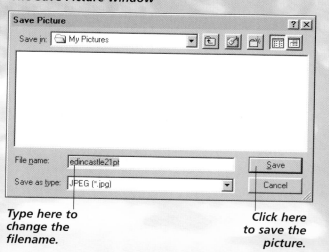

Type here to change the filename.

Click here to save the picture.

Placing pictures on your page

Once you have the pictures you want to use, it is easy to place them on your Web page. Make sure that they are not too big – the files should be under 40 kilobytes (KB) in size. If you are not sure how big a picture file is, you can check by opening up the My Pictures folder in My Documents and clicking on the file. In the left-hand part of the window you will see details of the file, including its size, as below.

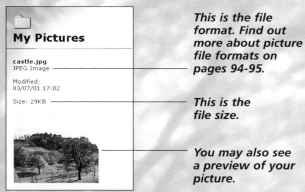

This is the file format. Find out more about picture file formats on pages 94-95.

This is the file size.

You may also see a preview of your picture.

Now open up your Web page in FrontPage. Choose where on the page you would like your picture to appear, place the cursor at the end of the line before and press the return key (to give the picture enough space between lines of text). Check that the cursor is in the right position on the page – you can place a picture on the left, the middle or the right of a page by clicking on the text alignment buttons in the formatting toolbar.

Click on these buttons to position the picture.

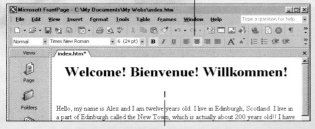

The cursor shows you the picture will be centred.

Now select the picture you want to use. Click on *Insert* in the menu bar and then on *Picture* and then *From File...* in the drop-down menu that appears. A window will appear like the one below.

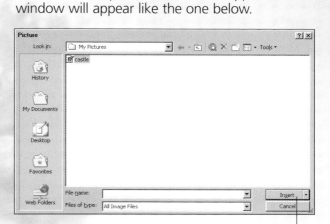

Click here to place your picture on the page.

Click on My Documents, open My Pictures and select your picture. Click on *Insert*, and FrontPage will place it on your Web page.

If you want to make the picture larger or smaller, click on it. You will see eight black dots around its edges. Click and drag one of the dots on the corners until the picture is the right size.

Finally, remember to insert a credit below the picture. (You can make the type a size or two smaller than your main text.)

This is how your page might look once you have inserted the picture and credit.

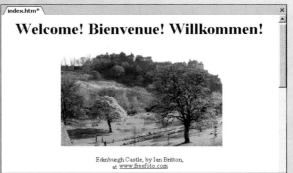

When you come to save your page, you will see that FrontPage also saves the picture separately into My Webs, as an "embedded file".

Backgrounds and colour

Coloured or patterned backgrounds are a popular way of making a Web page look brighter. You can use Microsoft® FrontPage® to add a simple coloured background, or search the Internet for a pattern you like. As with clip art, you will find thousands to choose from.

Changing the background colour

The default background (the standard one used until you make any changes) in FrontPage is white, and the text is black. Page 87 described one way of changing the text colour. You can also change default text and background colours by using the *Format Background* commands.

Open up your Web page in FrontPage. Click on *Format* in the menu bar, and a drop-down menu will appear. Click on *Background...* in this menu, and a Page Properties window will open like the one below.

Click here to change the background colour.

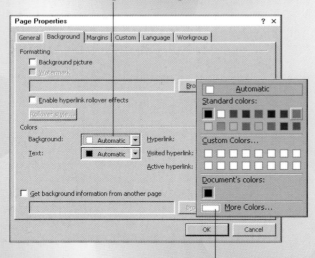

Click here to choose a new colour.

In the Colors section of the window, click on the box beside *Background* to change the background colour. As with the text, you will be offered a choice of sixteen standard colours, but you may prefer to mix your own. To do this, click on *More Colors...* in the box at the bottom of the colour menu.

Mixing a new colour

When you select *More Colors...*, you will see a window like the one below, with a choice of 133 more colours. Click on any of the hexagons to select that colour, and then click *OK*.

You can choose any of these colours.

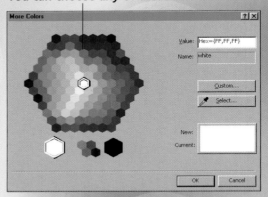

For a bigger range of colours still, click on *Custom...* to define your colour. A window will appear like the one below.

Select a colour from the spectrum...   **...and a shade from the bar on the right.**

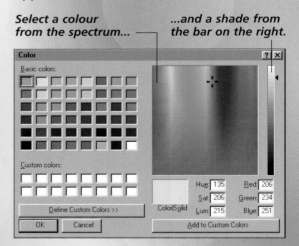

Click on the first box below *Custom Colors:* and then select a colour from the spectrum panel. You can make it darker or lighter by moving the black arrow beside the shade bar on the right. When you are happy with the colour, click on *Add to Custom Colors* and then on *OK*. You will return to the More Colors window; click on *OK*, and then *OK* again in the Page Properties window.

Changing the text colour

Your Web page might now look something like the first page below. You can also use the same method to change the default text colour, as on the second page.

Font colour has changed from black to dark blue.

Patterned backgrounds

You can find backgrounds on the Internet in the same way that you can find clip art. Try the sites below, or use a search engine (use the search terms **web design background**). Remember to credit the background designer and include a link to their page if they ask you to.

Backgrounds are fun to use, but choose them very carefully. A fussy, heavily-patterned background makes text difficult to read, and can actually make your page look *less* attractive.

Web sites for backgrounds

Go to **www.usborne-quicklinks.com** for links to collections of backgrounds, such as the huge range at **Barracuda Backgrounds**. There are patterns for all occasions at **The Background Boutique**, too.

Placing a background on your page

When you have found a background you like, save it into the My Pictures folder by right-clicking on it, as described for the clip art picture on page 88.

To place it on the page, go back to your page in FrontPage and click on *Format – Background...*, as you did on the page opposite for a plain-coloured background. In the Page Properties window which appears, click on the box next to *Background picture*, then click on the Browse button to locate the background you have saved.

Click here to select a background.

Click here to find the background image.

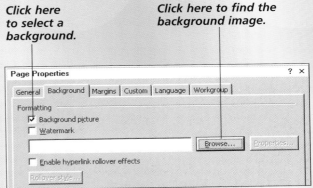

Find the file in My Pictures, as you did on page 89, and click *OK* and *OK* again. Your page will appear with its background, as below. When you save the page, FrontPage will also save the background image separately into My Webs.

This is the page with the background in place.

Adding pages and creating links

Once you know how to set up a Web page, you can easily create more pages and link them to the original.

Starting a new page

To create a new page in Microsoft® FrontPage®, all you have to do is click on the blank paper icon in the top left-hand corner of the screen. If you are working on an existing page, save it and close it first. Do this by clicking on *File – Save* and then *File – Close* in the menu bar. Then open a new page by clicking on the blank paper icon.

Click here to open a new page.

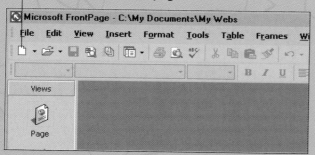

Save the page, as you did on page 85, and change its file name if you like. FrontPage will save the new page, as well as any new pictures, into My Webs.

You could create a page all about your home town.

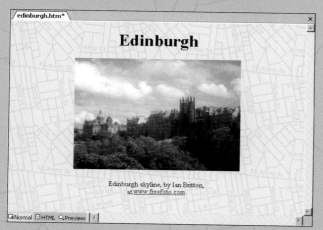

Creating a navigation structure

When you have more than one page for your site, you need to incorporate them in a structure which will keep all the pages together. You can do this by using the Navigation view in the Views bar to add on to your home page.

Click on Navigation at the left-hand side of the FrontPage window. You will see a window like the one below, with the Folder List on the left and an area on the right containing your home page. (The latest versions of FrontPage automatically place your new page in the same navigation structure as your home page, and you will see it in the area on the right as well.)

Click here to see your site's navigation structure.

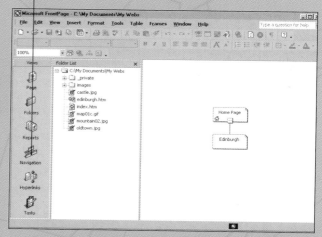

If you only see your home page in the area on the right, you will need to add your new page to the site's structure. Click on your new page in the Folders List, hold your mouse button down and drag it into the area on the right. You will see a grey line linking it to your home page. Make sure that your new page is below the home page, then release the mouse button.

You will now see both pages in the Navigation area, linked by a solid blue line. To go back and work on your page, click on Page in the Views bar.

You can create and add more pages to your site in the same way.

Linking to your new page

Once you have placed your new page in the navigation structure, you need to create a link to it from your home page.

Start by opening your home page. You can link either a word or a picture to your new page. Highlight the word you want to link, or select the picture, then click on the Hyperlink button in the Toolbar. An Insert Hyperlink window will appear.

Select the item you want to link, and click on this symbol to create a hyperlink.

This will be the link.

Click on your new page to link it.

In the list of files, click on the filename of your new page. The filename will appear in the *Address:* box. Click *OK*.

If you have linked a word to your new page, you will now see it in blue type and underlined. This shows visitors that it is a hyperlink.

Save your page. To see that the link is working, you can click on the Preview tab at the bottom left-hand corner of the FrontPage window. This shows you how your page will appear when published. When you click on the link, you will be taken directly to your new page.

Linking to another Web site

Links between pages of a Web site are called local links. Links from one Web site to another are called remote links, and you create them in much the same way.

For example, you might want to insert a hyperlink as part of a credit if you have used clip art or backgrounds from another Web site. First type in your credit (check the Web site to see if there is any specific wording you should use) and the URL of the site. Highlight the URL, and click on the Hyperlink button in the Toolbar. An Insert Hyperlink window will appear.

Type the site's URL into this box.

The hyperlink appears in blue and underlined.

Type the site's URL into the *Address* box – be sure to type it correctly – then click *OK*. The link will appear on your main page in blue and underlined. If you are online, you can check it using the Preview tab, as for a local link.

You can also make a picture into a remote link – you might do this if a site asks you to show its logo as part of a credit. Save the logo from the original site and place it as you would clip art (see page 89). Then click on it to select it, and create the hyperlink as above.

When you view the page using the Preview tab, you can tell that the logo is a hyperlink because your mouse cursor turns into a pointing hand when it is over the logo.

Preparing your own pictures

Once you know how to place pictures on your Web page, you can try using pictures of your own. To do this, you will need to prepare them as digital images that you can store on your computer. Digital images are pictures converted into number code that your computer reads in order to display the picture.

Image resolution

A picture on a computer is divided into tiny dots called pixels. Each pixel is one single colour, but they are so tiny that when you see the whole picture, the colours blend together smoothly. The digital image file tells your computer the exact colour and position of each pixel.

Pixels ——

This part of the picture has been enlarged so that you can see the pixels.

Digital images can be saved in different ways, and some picture file formats are more suitable for Web pages than others. The more pixels a picture is divided into, the more smoothly the colours blend. The number of pixels is known as resolution, and is measured in dots per inch (dpi).

A high-resolution picture looks very sharp and clear, but takes up a lot of memory space on a computer. A low-resolution picture takes up less space, but may look fuzzy. If you are printing a picture out on paper, you generally need to print at high resolution, but pictures on a Web page will look fine at a low resolution of 72 dpi.

On the right you can see the difference between a high-resolution and a low-resolution image.

Preparing digital images

There are several ways of creating digital images. If you create the image in a computer graphics program, such as Microsoft® Paint, it will automatically be saved in digital form. As long as you save it in the right file format (see opposite), you can then place it directly on a Web page.

If you have a digital camera, it will save the photos you take in digital form. You can download the photos from the camera to your computer, using the special software supplied with the camera. You can use the software to convert the picture into the right file format. You may also need to compress it by reducing the resolution.

A digital camera

You can also convert photographs or drawings you have into digital form by using a scanner. A scanner works a little like a photocopier, but produces a digital image file rather than an actual copy from your original. Top quality scanners for printing and publishing cost a lot of money, but

A scanner

you can buy inexpensive basic versions for home use. Many photocopying bureaux also have scanners that you can use for a small charge.

This is a high-resolution image. It was scanned in at 300 dpi.

This is a low-resolution image. It was scanned in at 72 dpi.

Picture file format

The more memory space a picture uses, the longer it will take to download on a Web page. To save downloading time, picture files are either simplified or compressed (made smaller).

Two of the commonest picture file formats for Web pages are GIF files and JPEG files. GIF files are good for simple pictures in basic colours, such as cartoons, as they keep files small by using a maximum of 256 colours. GIF files are also good for icons – small pictures which represent something else, such as a link to another part of your site.

These icons are GIF files. GIF files are suitable for simple images using a limited range of colours.

JPEG files are often used for photographs and pictures with a lot of detail, as they can include more colours than GIFs but can be compressed to take up very little space.

These are JPEG images. JPEG files are best for complex images, such as photographs.

Saving files as GIFs

When you save a picture in a graphics program, you can choose to save it as a GIF. When you click on *File* and then *Save As...*, you will see a Save As window like the one below. In the box *Save as type*, select GIF (or Graphics Interchange Format) from the options you are given. Your image file will have a file name ending in .gif

The Save As window

Select GIF as the file type here.

Saving files as JPEGs

You can save a picture as a JPEG in the same way, by selecting the file type JPEG (or JPEG File Interchange Format). Your file will have a name ending in .jpg

Some graphics programs allow you to alter the amount a JPEG file is compressed. This means that you can make the file smaller, but the image quality won't be quite as good. Try saving different versions of your picture, compressed by different amounts. When you place the picture on your Web page, use the Preview tab to see what it will look like. Use the smallest sized file that still looks good. In any case, try to keep picture files under 40KB in size.

Using your pictures

You can place your pictures on your Web page in the same way as you placed clip art on pages 88-89. These pages will also show you a few more ways you can use pictures to make your page more interesting.

Creating a hotspot

With Microsoft® FrontPage®, you can choose to make just one area of a picture into a hyperlink. For example, the page below is a welcome page for a band Web site. To reach the rest of the site, you have to click on the bird in the logo (which has been saved as a GIF file).

Click on the image and use one of these three buttons to create a hotspot.

Place your picture, then click on it to select it. Click on one of the Create Hotspot buttons in the Pictures toolbar at the bottom of the screen. If you are using the rectangular or circular hotspot buttons, click at one corner of the area you want to make into a hotspot, and drag the cursor until you have enclosed the area. If you are using the polygonal hotspot button, click on points all around the area you want to enclose.

When you have fully enclosed your hotspot area, a Create Hyperlink window will appear, as on page 93. Select the Web page you want to link to, and click *OK*.

Using icons

Icons are a great way of making a Web page look brighter without making it take a long time to download. This makes them especially useful on a home page, which should download quickly but still look attractive.

You can either use icons from a clip art gallery (see page 88 for the names of some clip art sites), or create your own. Try creating simple icons in a graphics program such as Microsoft® Paint, or scan in simple drawings and save them as GIF files. Keep them small – they should appear on your Web page at about 15mm^2.

The home page below uses home-produced icons as hyperlinks to other areas of the site. The hyperlinks are also given in words, in case the icon meanings aren't clear. You make the icons and their descriptions into hyperlinks in the same way as on page 93.

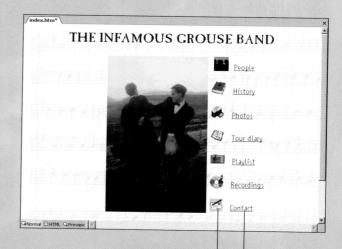

Both the icons and their descriptions act as hyperlinks to other pages on the site.

The page also includes a home-produced background (hand-written sheet music, scanned in and saved as a GIF file) and a single photo. You can find out how to place a photo with text beside it like this on the page opposite.

Wrapping text around a picture

When you tried placing a picture on page 89, you had the option of placing it on the left, in the middle or on the right of your Web page. If you place a picture in this way, you will find that you can't place more than one line of text alongside it. If you want to place a picture in text, as on the page below, you need to tell FrontPage to wrap the text around it.

This page has text wrapped around a picture.

Open your page of text, and place the picture at the beginning of the main text block. Click on the picture to select it, then click on *Format* in the Menu bar and then *Position...* from the drop-down menu which appears. You will see a window like the one below. Under *Wrapping style*, click on *Left,* and your picture will be positioned to the left of your text. You can then adjust the picture size by clicking and dragging the points at its corners, until you are happy with the look of your page.

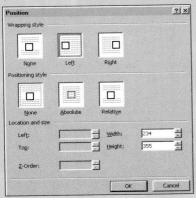

The text wrap Position window

Creating a picture gallery

You might like to show a collection of pictures together on a picture gallery page. Normally, if you put too many pictures together on a page, it makes the page very slow to download. You can avoid this, though, by showing the pictures in mini versions called thumbnails. If you click on a thumbnail, another page will open showing a full-sized version.

FrontPage makes it easy to create thumbnails. First, place all the pictures you want on your picture gallery page. Click on a picture to select it, and then click on the Auto Thumbnail button in the Pictures toolbar at the bottom of the screen. FrontPage will turn the picture into a thumbnail, with a blue outline which shows that it is a hyperlink (to the page with the full-sized version of the picture). You can resize the thumbnail as you would a normal picture, by clicking and dragging the corner points.

When you come to save the page, FrontPage will also save both versions of each image – the thumbnail and the full-size version.

Click here to turn an image into a thumbnail.

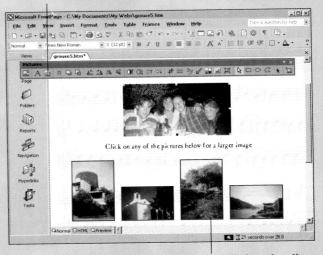

These four images are all thumbnails.

User-friendly Web pages

You can add elements to your site to make it more welcoming and easy to navigate. For example, you can create a special link to allow visitors to e-mail you, or add a counter to track visits. You can also help visitors to find your site, and find their way around when they get there.

Creating an e-mail link

Many Web sites include a link that people can click on to contact the site owner. Generally, this is via e-mail, although commercial Web sites may also include business addresses and phone numbers. Clicking on an e-mail link creates an e-mail pre-addressed to you, which your visitors can then complete and send.

In Microsoft® FrontPage®, you create an e-mail link in much the same way as you create any hyperlink (see pages 92-93). Highlight the text or select the icon you want to make into an e-mail link, then click on the Create Hyperlink button in the Toolbar. An Insert Hyperlink window will appear. Click on the small envelope symbol at the bottom of the window, and an E-mail Address window will appear over the Insert Hyperlink window. Type your e-mail address, then click *OK*.

Click here to create an e-mail link.

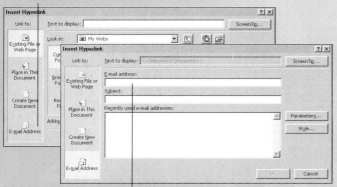

Type your e-mail address in this box.

To see the link working, click on the Preview tab at the bottom of the main FrontPage window, then click on your e-mail link. Like your visitors, you will see a blank e-mail pre-addressed to you.

⚠ Nuisance e-mail

Remember, if you put an e-mail address on your Web site, anyone at all who sees your site can use it. There is a risk that people might send you rude or annoying messages.

Before you create an e-mail link, see whether your e-mail account has a facility for filtering or blocking messages from nuisance senders. Never reply to a nuisance message, just delete it and block the sender.

Inserting a hit counter

A hit counter is a popular way of keeping track of visits to your site: it's fun to be able to see on the site itself how many visits it has received. FrontPage includes several styles of hit counter you can choose from, and it's easy to place one on your home page. You will only be able to use one if your ISP supports FrontPage Extensions, though (find out more about FrontPage Extensions on page 105).

Place the cursor on your home page where you want the counter to appear. You could introduce it with the words "You are visitor number", or something similar. Then click on *Insert* in the Menu bar, and then on *Web*

component and then *Hit Counter* in the menus which appear. Choose the counter style you prefer, and click *Finish* and then *OK*.

You can choose from these counter styles in FrontPage.

On your page, you will see the words [Hit Counter] but, even when you use the Preview tab, you will not actually see the counter yet. It will appear when you come to publish your page on the Internet.

Inserting keywords

When you publish your Web site, you can arrange for more people to see it by submitting it to a few search engines. Most search engines find sites by looking for keywords – words which describe what the site is all about. These don't appear as such on the site, but are hidden in the HTML code near the top of the page, where a search engine can find them easily.

You'll find more about submitting your site to search engines on page 109, but it's a good idea to insert keywords at this stage, before you publish your site. Search engines generally allow up to fifteen keywords. You can choose keywords for each page of your site, if you like (different pages will then show as results for different search terms), or just for your home page.

To insert keywords, first open your page. Click on *File* in the menu bar and then on *Properties* in the drop-down menu which appears. Click on the Custom tab in the Page Properties window which appears. In the *User variables* section, click on *Add...* You will see a window like the one below.

Type keywords *in this box*

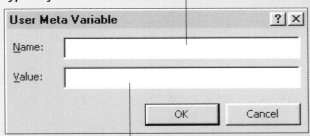

Type your keywords in here, separated by commas.

In the *Name* box, type **keywords**. In the *Value* box, type your keywords, separated by commas. Then click *OK*, and then *OK* again.

You will not see the keywords on your page in the Normal page view, but you can check that they are there by clicking on the HTML tab at the bottom left-hand corner of the FrontPage window. About five or six lines from the top, you will see `<meta name="keywords" content=` with the keywords you have chosen.

Setting bookmarks

You can set up a hyperlink within a single page of your Web site. On a long page, for example, it's useful for visitors to be able to go back to the top of the page quickly. Show visitors that they can do this by using an icon of an upward-pointing arrow, or the words "Back to top", at the bottom of your page.

To create the link, first place the cursor at the top of the page. Click on *Insert* in the Toolbar, and then on *Bookmark...* in the drop-down menu that appears. You will see a window like the one below.

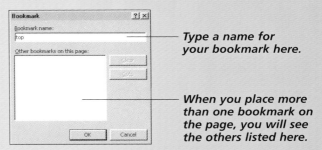

Type a name for your bookmark here.

When you place more than one bookmark on the page, you will see the others listed here.

Give your bookmark a name, then click *OK*. At the top of your page you will now see a little flag symbol (this will not show on the finished page).

Now insert your arrow icon or link words at the bottom of your page. Make them into a hyperlink, as on page 92. In the Insert Hyperlink window, click on the *Bookmark* option.

Click here, then select your bookmark name.

You can place more than one bookmark on a page, if you like. Another neat way of using bookmarks is to have a list of contents at the top of a page, with each item in the list linked to a bookmark further down the page.

Collecting information

If you want to find out more about your visitors, you can create a form on your Web site to gather details. Forms can be used to ask for feedback or take membership details for clubs or societies. They are also used to take personal and financial details on a commercial Web site – many of the processes involved are the same.

Forms are easy to place in Microsoft® FrontPage®, although they are FrontPage components, so you need to make sure your Web hosting company supports FrontPage Extensions (see page 105).

Placing a form on a page

In FrontPage, you create a basic form on a Web page by positioning your cursor on the page and clicking *Insert* – *Form* – *Form*. On your page, you will see a rectangle with a dotted outline, like the one below. (The dotted line will not appear on the finished page.)

```
grouse10.htm*                                    ×

                    Feedback

Please tell us a little about yourself and help us to improve our site:
┌─────────────────────────────────────────────┐
│ Submit │ Reset │                              │
│                                               │
│                                               │
│                                               │
│                         🏠 Home               │
└─────────────────────────────────────────────┘
```

You add elements to this form to collect different kinds of information.

Almost all forms on the Internet contain Submit and Reset buttons, so these are included automatically in the FrontPage form. Your visitors will click on Submit to send the completed form to you, and Reset to clear the form if they want to make changes to the details they have given.

Now you can add boxes to your form to collect different kinds of information.*

Names and addresses

FrontPage allows you to collect information in various different ways. For example, if you want to know someone's name and e-mail address, you can just give them a short text box in which they can type the information you need.

First type what it is you're asking for. This is known as a prompt (for example, "Your name:"). Then click on *Insert* – *Form* – *Textbox*, and click Return. You can do this for as many entries as you like.

```
Please tell us a little about yourself and help us to improve our site:

Your name: [                    ]

E-mail: [                    ]

[Submit] [Reset]
```

Use one-line text boxes for visitors to type in short items, such as e-mail addresses.

Radio buttons

Radio buttons, or option buttons, allow visitors to choose one of several options, for example a particular age range. You can click on any item in a list, but only one item can be selected at a time.

Type your list of prompts, and after each item in the list click on *Insert* – *Form* – *Option button*. After each prompt, click Tab or Return to separate the items so that it is clear which button belongs to which item. For each group of prompts with radio buttons, FrontPage will only allow one button to be selected at a time.

```
Please tell us a little about yourself and help us to improve our site:

Your name: [                    ]

E-mail: [                    ]

Your age: under 16 ⦿  16-24 ○  25-34 ○  35 and over ○

[Submit] [Reset]
```

Radio buttons allow visitors to select just one option.

*Under the 1998 Data Protection Act in the UK, you may collect "personal data" such as names and e-mail addresses for your own personal, recreational use only. If you are using the data for any other purposes, you should refer to the Office of the Information Commissioner.

Check boxes

Radio buttons only allow visitors to select one option, and one option must always be selected. However, you may want to allow several items in a list to be selected – in a list of hobbies, for example. You may also want an option which can be left unselected – if you are offering to send someone information, maybe. You can do this by using check boxes.

Type your prompt or prompts, as for radio buttons. After each one, click *Insert – Form – Checkbox*. Visitors can click on the box to select it, and click again to clear it.

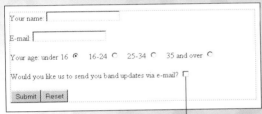

Visitors can choose whether or not to select this option.

Scrolling text boxes

If you want to give visitors more than one line space to type text – for example, if you are asking for their comments – you can insert a text box which gives them as much room as they need. Type your prompt, then click *Insert – Form – Text Area* (or *Scrolling Text Box*). The box that appears on the page is quite small, but if you click on it you will see eight black points around the edges, and you can drag any of these points to make the box wider or longer.

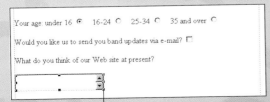

Click and drag these points if you want to expand your text box.

Processing the information

Once you have finished your form, save your page. You can format the form as you would any other text – changing the font, size, position of items and so on. You can see how it will look on the finished page by using the Preview tab, as on page 102.

Now you need to arrange for the information you collect to be processed and sent back to you. You will only be sent whatever your visitors type on the page, so in order to make sense of the results, it helps to give a name to each entry, or form field.

To do this, right-click on a form field, for example the one-line text box next to "Your name:". In the menu that appears, click on *Form Field Properties...* The *Name:* box has the default name T1, but it makes sense to change this to "Name". Click *OK*. Then do the same for the box next to "E-mail:", naming it "E-mail", and so on.

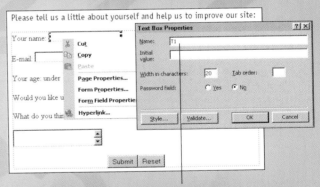

Give a name to each form field. Radio buttons have a group name: give the same name to each button in the group.

Finally, you can arrange for the results to be sent to you. FrontPage includes a device called a form handler which automatically sends results to a file in the _private folder of your Web structure. However, it may be more convenient for you to receive results via e-mail. To do this, right-click anywhere on the form and click on *Form Properties*. In the window that appears, type your e-mail address in the *E-mail address* box, then click *OK*.

Checking your site

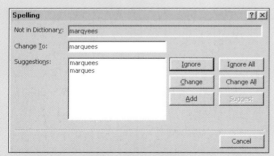

Pages 80-101 of this book contained a selection of techniques to help you to put together a basic Web site with some fun and interesting features. Once you have put your site together, you are almost ready to publish it on the Internet. Before you do that, though, it's really important to check all the pages thoroughly.

Checking spelling

One check you should always carry out is of the spelling on your pages – a Web site with spelling mistakes looks really sloppy. Microsoft® FrontPage® includes a spell checker, which you'll find under *Tools* in the Menu bar. You may have seen wiggly red underlinings in your text, and corrected any errors already, but it's worth running a final check.

You don't need to highlight text, if you click on *Tools* and then *Spelling...* the spell checker will check all text on the page, highlighting possible errors and suggesting alternatives. When FrontPage finds an unfamiliar word, a window will appear like the one below.

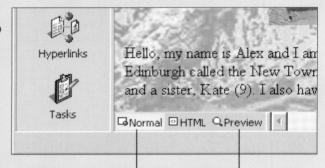

FrontPage provides alternatives for unfamiliar words which may be errors.

You can choose to *Ignore* the suggested alternatives (or *Ignore All* if the word appears more than once on the page), or select an alternative and *Change* (or *Change All*) if the word is actually wrong. You can also *Add* the word to FrontPage's dictionary if it is something like a surname that you expect to use again. When the check is complete, you will get a message telling you so.

Using the Preview tab

Page 93 showed you how to use the Preview tab to see how elements would look on your finished page. It's important to check all your pages like this, as there may be slight differences between the look of a page when you are editing it (in the Normal window) and when it is published (as in the Preview window).

You can click on one tab or another at the bottom left-hand corner of your browser window. This makes it easy to go back to the Normal page view if you need to make any changes.

You can switch between Normal and Preview windows by clicking on these tabs.

Previewing in your browser

You can also use the Preview in Browser command to view your page. This is particularly useful for checking hyperlinks, as you can simply use your browser's Back and Forward buttons to go quickly from one page to another.

Click on *File* in the Menu bar, and then *Preview in Browser...* from the drop-down menu that appears. A window will appear with your browser's name and a choice of window sizes, related to different screen sizes. Choose *Default* to select your own screen size, or choose a smaller size to make sure your page will still look good. Most screens these days can display Web pages at 800x600, so check your pages at that size if your own screen size is any different.

Checking links

There are other ways of checking the links between pages. You can see a map of the links to and from a particular page by clicking on Hyperlinks in the Views bar on the left of the FrontPage window. You might see something like the map below.

This shows the links to and from a home page.

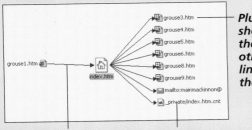

Plus signs show that there are other pages linked to these ones.

Unbroken blue arrows show working links.

This is a hit counter.

On this map, local links will show as file names, global links as URLs and mail links as e-mail addresses. Working links will show as straight blue arrows, broken links as broken red arrows. Check and fix any broken links you see.

Downloading time

You may have noticed a little hourglass and a time in seconds at the bottom right-hand corner of the FrontPage window. This tells you approximately how long your page will take to download at various modem speeds. It isn't altogether reliable, but gives you a good idea. Ideally, you want your opening page or a home page to download in under 30 seconds – any longer will be frustrating for your visitors.

If you want to reset the modem speed, click on the time given and then click on a different speed in the list which appears.

Click here to change the modem speed.

Renaming pages

It may be that once you have created a few pages, you decide it makes sense to rename one or more of them. Don't just rename pages by changing their filenames in the My Webs folder of My Documents, though. Use FrontPage to change the filenames, and all files and links associated with those pages will be updated too.

Click on Folders in the Views bar, and you will see a list like the one below. Click on a page to select it, pause and then click again on the filename (if you click again immediately FrontPage will just open the page). You can now change your filename, and FrontPage will show you a message if there are any links on other pages which need to be updated. Click *OK* to update these links.

This is the Folders list.

Don't delete or rename these two folders. They may be used by FrontPage to store information when your site is published.

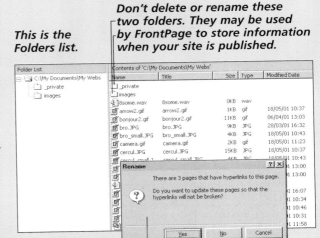

This message appears when links on other pages need updating.

A second opinion

Once your site is ready and you have checked all the links, try asking a friend to give it one last check. Do this using the *Preview in Browser...* command, as described on the page opposite, so that they can follow any links easily. They may notice things you have missed, or be able to suggest some improvements.

Ways to publish your site

To publish your site on the Internet, you need to copy it to a server or host computer which will store it and make it available for people to visit. This copying process is called uploading. You can choose between different hosting options.

Servers

A server

Servers are powerful computers which have huge amounts of memory for storing Web sites. They are always switched on, so people can access sites at any time of day, from anywhere in the world. Servers are generally owned and maintained by specialist companies. These companies sell or rent out space to businesses and individuals for their Web sites.

Hosting companies make use of high-speed connections to the Internet, such as satellite and fibre-optic cable. In theory this means your site should download more quickly; in practice your visitors will see more of a difference if they have a high-speed connection themselves. It's worth visiting the hosting company's home page to see how quickly their own site downloads, but avoid paying extra for high-speed connection services if most of your visitors are unlikely to benefit.

Web space with your ISP

If you have an account with an ISP, your easiest option may be to use the Web space provided by them. Your domain name will be allocated by your ISP; usually it is based on the username you chose when you first signed up. To find out how to upload your site, go to your ISP's Web site and look for instructions in the Members section or the Help section.

The amount of space offered by most ISPs is limited to about 10 or 15 MB, but this should be more than enough for most personal sites. If you find that your site is bigger than that (for example, if it includes a lot of sound clips or animations), you will find more space with a Web-based hosting company. You can check the size of your site in Microsoft® FrontPage® by using the Reports command. (Find out how to do this on page 106.)

These are the logos of ISPs from different countries.

Your own domain name

You can choose and register your own URL ending in .com, .co.uk, .org, .net etc. This is known as domain name registration; your domain name is the name part of your URL, for example Usborne in www.usborne.com. Every URL is unique, so you have to choose a name which has not already been registered by someone else, although you may be able to use the same name with a different ending (www.name.net instead of www.name.com, for example).

Your ISP may offer a domain name registration service, and you often see them advertised in computer magazines. You will have to pay a fee to register the name for a set period (one year, two years, five...), and another fee for hosting your site. Sometimes the registration and hosting fees are combined in the same package.

Web-based hosting

If you build your site on someone else's computer, for example at a library or Internet café, you will need to find a hosting company, or Web Presence Provider, on the Internet. There are a number of Web-based companies that host Web sites free of charge. They generally cover their costs by including advertising on your site. The advertising usually appears as a banner across the top of your page, or a pop-up window which you can close.

Well known Web-based hosting companies include Geocities, now part of the Yahoo!® network, and Angelfire and Tripod, now part of the Lycos® network. Their sites offer help with Web page building, using predesigned templates, but you can also upload a site you have designed yourself.

You will need to sign up as a member to use Web hosting facilities. You can do this quickly and easily on the hosting company's Web site.

These are some popular Web-based hosting companies.

Web hosting services

If you are looking for a Web hosting company, you'll find links to some of the best-known at the Usborne Quicklinks site, **www.usborne-quicklinks.com**

If you want to find a free Web hosting company that supports FrontPage Extensions, try the **Web hosting** page of the **free frontpage stuff** Web site.

You can also find links to **Geocities**, **Tripod**, **Angelfire** and others on the Quicklinks site.

Some hosting companies operate worldwide; others have different pages for the US, the UK and other countries. This means that they can make more domain names available, because the same name can be used with different endings for different countries.

FrontPage Extensions

The easiest way to publish a Web site created with FrontPage is to use the *Publish Web...* command in the *File* menu. To do this, you need to find a Web Presence Provider that supports FrontPage Extensions, or has FrontPage Server Extensions installed.

Without FrontPage Server Extensions, some elements on your Web site may not work. This is true of most inserted components, such as hit counters (see page 98) and forms (see pages 100-101). FrontPage Server Extensions also make it easier for you to edit your site using FrontPage at a later date. When you upload your revised files, FrontPage will compare the revised and original versions and update any links as necessary.

You can find a list of Web Presence Providers that support FrontPage Extensions by opening FrontPage and clicking on *File – Publish Web... – WPP's*, which connects you to a page of the Microsoft Web site. Click on Locate an International WPP if you are outside the US or Canada. Most of these companies charge a fee for Web hosting services, but you can find some free ones – see the box on the left.

What if my ISP doesn't support FrontPage Extensions?

You can still upload a site to an ISP without FrontPage Extensions, but you will have to make sure that your site doesn't contain any forms or components such as hit counters. In order to upload your site, you use FTP (File Transfer Protocol). You can find out more about this on page 107.

Uploading your site

Once you have checked your site thoroughly, and decided on a company to host it, you are ready to upload. If your hosting company supports FrontPage Extensions, you can use the *Publish Web...* command. Otherwise you can upload your site using FTP. Both methods are described here.

A final check

Before you publish your page, you should run one last check to be sure that all the links are working, and to see how big the files are. This will tell you how much Web space your site needs.

The best way to do this in Microsoft® FrontPage® is to use the Reports command. Open your home page and click on *View – Reports*. Click on *Site Summary* in the menu that appears. You will see a table like the one below.

This figure shows the total size of your site.

Name	Count	Size	Description
All files	56	467KB	All files in the current Web
Pictures	39	414KB	Picture files in the current Web (GIF, JPG, BMP, et
Unlinked files	15	250KB	Files in the current Web that cannot be reached by
Linked files	41	218KB	Files in the current Web that can be reached by st
Slow pages	2	128KB	Pages in the current Web exceeding an estimated
Older files	22	296KB	Files in the current Web that have not been modifi
Recently added fi...	2	3KB	Files in the current Web that have been created in
Hyperlinks	89		All hyperlinks in the current Web
Unverified hyperli...	20		Hyperlinks pointing to unconfirmed target files
Broken hyperlinks	1		Hyperlinks pointing to unavailable target files
External hyperlinks	20		Hyperlinks pointing to files outside of the current W
Internal hyperlinks	69		Hyperlinks pointing to other files within the current
Component errors	2		Files in the current Web with components reportin
Uncompleted tasks	0		Tasks in the current Web that are not yet marked
Unused themes	0		Themes in the current Web that are not applied to

How big is your site?

In the top row, under Size, you will see a figure which tells you the total size of the files on your site. If your site will be hosted by your ISP, check that this is within the limit the ISP has set. For most personal sites, this is not a problem. If your site is over the limit, you may have to edit your site or choose an alternative host.

Slow pages

In the row entitled Slow pages, you will see whether there are any pages which will take longer than 30 seconds to download over a 28K modem. Double-click on this row to see which they are.

Make sure that your home page, at least, doesn't take this long to download. You can edit other pages by including fewer picture files, or by creating extra pages and sharing content between them.

You may decide that it doesn't matter if some pages are slow to download. Most people today have modems faster than 28K, but you should still try to limit the number of slow pages as visitors do find them very frustrating.

Hyperlinks

You will see several rows relating to hyperlinks. In the row entitled Unverified hyperlinks, you may see a figure. This means that FrontPage has not tested the link to see that it connects to the right destination. To verify all your hyperlinks, click on *View – Toolbars – Reporting*. You will see a toolbar like the one below. Click on the hyperlink symbol at the right-hand side of this bar. FrontPage will check all your hyperlinks and report any problems.

In the Reports view, you will also see a row entitled Broken hyperlinks. If you run the Verify Hyperlinks check as described above, this should highlight any broken links, which you can then remove or restore.

Click here to verify hyperlinks.

Ready to upload

To upload your site to a host with FrontPage Server Extensions, first make sure you are online. Then open your home page and click on *File – Publish Web...* You will see a window like the one below.

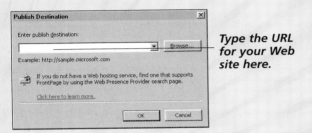

Type the URL for your Web site here.

In the box, type the URL allocated to your Web site by your ISP or hosting company. Then click on *Publish*. You may have to wait a minute or two for FrontPage to locate your ISP or host.

You will then be asked to give your name and password. This is the username and password you selected when you signed up with your ISP or hosting company.

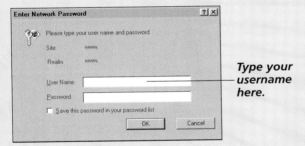

Type your username here.

FrontPage will then start uploading the pages of your site to your ISP or host. This, too, could take a few minutes. When it is done, you will see a message like the one below. Click on the underlined text to see your published site.

This message tells you your site has been published.

Using FTP

If your host doesn't support FrontPage Server Extensions, you will need to use FTP (File Transfer Protocol) to publish your site. To do this, you will need an FTP client program. Your ISP may offer you a copy, or you can find one easily on the Internet (you can find links to useful Web sites at **www.usborne-quicklinks.com**).

Open your FTP client program. The program used in these examples is called Terrapin FTP. First you need to set up a connection with your ISP's server. Click on *Server – New Connection* and type the server address of your ISP's Web server (your ISP will tell you what this is). Type your username and password, and click on *Connect*.

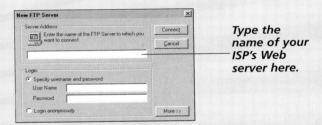

Type the name of your ISP's Web server here.

Once you have established a connection, you will see a window divided into two parts. The top part shows your ISP's server, the bottom part is your own computer. Simply select the files which make up your Web site (remember to select all the image files as well) and drag them into the top window. Your FTP client program will then copy them to your ISP's server.

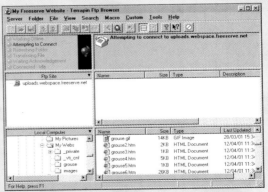

Select and drag files from the bottom window to the top one.

Maintaining and updating your site

Once your site is published, it's important to review it regularly and keep it up to date. You may have additions or improvements to make, or you may find that some of your links break down and need updating or replacing.

Checking your site

Use your own and other computers to visit your site from time to time. You may find that the site looks different when viewed using a different computer, screen size or browser – for example, colours on a Macintosh computer appear brighter than on a PC. Ask other people's opinions, too.

Perhaps the most important details to check for are broken links and pages that are slow to download. Both of these are very frustrating for visitors, so try to fix them quickly. You can either check these by visiting your page or by using the Reports command, as described on page 106.

Adding a date

If you plan to update your site regularly, it's a good idea to make a feature of the date so that your visitors can see just how current the page is. Using Microsoft® FrontPage®, you can easily add a line of text at the bottom of your home page, then insert the date by clicking on *Insert – Date and Time...* Each time you go back to edit the page, this line will be updated.

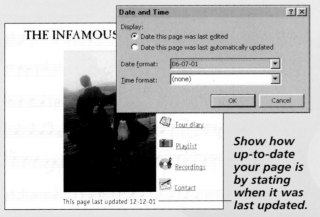

Show how up-to-date your page is by stating when it was last updated.

Deleting unwanted files

When you've worked on your site a little, you may find that the Site Summary (see page 106) includes files you no longer plan to use. These may be images you have since replaced, or components you have decided not to have on the site.

If you want to get rid of them altogether, use the Reports view to list them – click on *View – Reports – All Files*. Click on the file or files to select them, then press Delete. You will get a message asking whether you are sure you want to delete. Click on *Yes* if you are sure.

The file and all links to it will be deleted, so make sure you check for broken hyperlinks (see page 106) before you upload your updated site.

Files you don't want to publish

If you don't want to delete files altogether, save them in FrontPage but mark them as not to be published. You can then use them again in later versions of your site if you want. Click on *View – Reports – Workflow – Publish Status*. You will see a list of files similar to the *All Files* list. Right-click on a file and then click on *Don't Publish*. (In older versions of FrontPage, click on *Properties...* and then click on the Workgroup tab; click in the box next to *Exclude this file when publishing the rest of the Web*, then click *OK*.)

The red cross symbol shows you that the file will not be uploaded when you come to update your site.

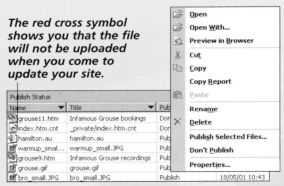

The file will be saved, but will not be uploaded to your Web server.

Updating your site

If you use the *Publish Web...* command in FrontPage to upload your site, it's easy to make changes and publish the latest version. Open a page of your site and click on *File – Publish Web...* You will see a window like the one below, with your site's URL already filled in.

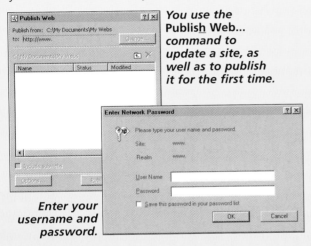

You use the **Publish Web...** *command to update a site, as well as to publish it for the first time.*

Enter your username and password.

You will be asked to give your username and password, as you did when you first published the site (see page 107). FrontPage will then compare the version of your site on your own computer with the version on your hosting company's server, and upload any updated pages. When the uploading process is complete, you will get a message to tell you so. However, it may take a day before you can view your updated site on the Internet.

Updating your site using FTP

If you used FTP to upload your site, as described on page 107, all you have to do is to open your FTP client program and wait until it has established a connection with your ISP or Web server. Then drag your updated files from the bottom part of the FTP client program window (representing your computer) to the top (representing your ISP). Your FTP client will automatically replace the older files with your updated versions.

Publicizing your site

When you are satisfied with your site, you'll want to encourage people to visit. Start by telling friends about the site – you can send them the URL in an e-mail.

To make your site more widely known, the best approach is to submit it to one or more search engines. Yahoo!®, for example, has a special category for personal home pages. You'll find a list of search engines in the box below.

Most search engines have a form you can use to tell them about your site. Their staff will then generally check your site before listing it (the check may take a few weeks, as so many new Web sites are created every day). Alternatively, you can use a service that automatically submits your site to a number of search engines.

To submit a site to Yahoo!, use the directory to go to the category you think is most suitable for your site, for example **Society and Culture – People – Personal Home Pages**. Click on "Suggest a Site" at the bottom of the page, and you will be taken through a simple four-step submission procedure, in which you give details of your site, a brief description and your own contact details. Once submitted, your site will be checked and then listed in the directory.

Search engines

Go to **www.usborne-quicklinks.com** for links to some of the most popular search engines, such as **Yahoo!®**, **Lycos®** and **Google**SM.

Some of these have different search engines for different countries, so choose whether you want to submit to the main US-based site or to the sites for the UK or other countries.

You'll also find links to the **AddMe** and **Submit Express** Web sites, which offer services including submitting sites free of charge to a range of search engines.

Internet future

The Internet is developing all the time. More and more people are getting connected to it and companies are creating products that make it easier to use. The most popular Internet facilities, such as e-mail and the World Wide Web, may not change much in the near future, but it will almost certainly become quicker, easier and less expensive to connect to them.

High-speed connections

High-speed Internet access, also known as broadband, is becoming more widely available and less expensive. The same technology which brings you cable TV can also offer fast Internet access. A cable modem can download data at around 512K, almost ten times as fast as a dial-up (telephone) modem. DSL (Digital Subscriber Line) technology uses existing telephone lines to transfer data up to 40 times as fast as a dial-up modem, although at present it is still too expensive for most home users.

Both cable and DSL connections are "always on", so that you don't have to wait for your modem to connect each time you log on to the Internet. This does mean that you are more at risk from hackers, so it is a good idea to install a "personal firewall" – software which prevents unauthorized access to your computer. However, it makes using the Internet far faster and easier, and makes it possible to include high-quality graphics, sound and video on Web sites which would take too long to download using a dial-up connection.

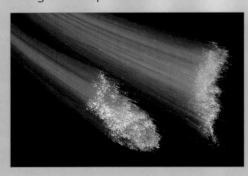

Fibre optic cables can transmit large amounts of data at high speed.

Internet entertainment

When broadband access becomes more widespread, there will be a range of services available to take advantage of it. You might select and download a film in minutes, just as you would choose a video – but with the Internet you could choose from a huge range of titles without even leaving home. There are also plans to show major sporting events as Webcasts (see page 65). With a basic 56K modem connection, picture download speed and quality are rarely high enough to show sports matches clearly, but they will be much better through a high-speed connection.

With broadband connections, it will be possible to show major sports matches as Webcasts.

Internet on the move

The Internet is no longer limited to computers – more and more everyday objects are being designed to connect and make use of Internet services. For example, the French car manufacturer Citroën has developed a car featuring a voice-controlled computer. As well as playing radio and CDs, it includes a navigation system, a mobile phone and e-mail, and can download traffic and weather reports. Other models in development include a multimedia car, with a PC, mobile phone and television installed in the back, so that passengers can work or be entertained while they travel.

This car has a voice-activated computer which can send and receive e-mail and download travel information.

Internet around the house

"Smart" home appliances could use the Internet to shop online or send messages to their owners.

A number of manufacturers are working on connecting home appliances, such as refrigerators and microwave ovens, to the Internet. A microwave, for example, could download recipes and cooking instructions from the Internet, while a refrigerator could order any fresh ingredients needed from an online supermarket. An Internet-connected washing machine could re-order washing powder when it was running low, and automatically report a fault to its owner or to the manufacturer's service centre. Even a garden sprinkler could download weather information to tell it when to water the lawn.

You could also use the Internet to keep an eye on your home, to let a friend or relative into the house while you are away, or to allow a delivery service access to the garage – perhaps to leave the groceries your smart appliances had ordered. It may sound like science fiction, but smart appliances are already being tested in homes in Denmark, Sweden and Singapore, and could be generally available in the next few years.

A panel in the door of this refrigerator can display recipe pages from the Internet.

Managing your life online

One Internet development which could show results very soon is Microsoft®'s HailStorm project. This is a way of storing personal information securely online, and then releasing the information only as and when necessary.

For example, if you wanted to book a flight online, HailStorm would already know if you had a preferred airline, and could arrange secure payment for the flight and enter it into your personal calendar, which you could access from your PC or mobile phone. If the flight were delayed, the information would automatically be sent to your personal calendar. If someone were meeting you at the airport, your arrival time could be forwarded to them – and they, too, would be informed if your flight were late.

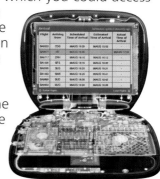

If HailStorm proves entirely secure, it could reassure many people about putting their personal details online, and lead to a huge increase in commercial use of the Internet.

Find out more

Find direct links to all these sites at **www.usborne-quicklinks.com**

There's a fascinating look into the future with one of the world's leading experts on the World Wide Web, Jakob Nielsen, on the **Internet Magazine** Web site.

Find out more about **Citroën**'s Internet-connected cars on their Web site.

Many Internet-connected appliances are first presented at the annual Consumer Electronics Show in the US. The **Howstuffworks** Web site has a guide to some of the amazing devices to be found there.

You can find a basic explanation of HailStorm on the **searchWin2000** site.

Mobile Internet

One of the most exciting developments in the way we use the Internet is that we can now connect on the move, using PDAs or mobile phones. Wireless and mobile Internet communications are developing fast, and can already offer some amazing services which will soon be much more widely available.

PDAs

PDAs (Personal Digital Assistants) have been popular for some years as digital diaries and address books. Some can also connect to laptop or desktop computers and transfer files, making it possible to work on documents on the move. Some PDAs are designed to work with mobile phones, and have a small keyboard and LCD screen. Others don't have a keyboard, and instead you use a special pen called a "stylus" to enter data on a touch-sensitive screen.

This PDA has a small keyboard attached.

Today, many PDAs can connect to the Internet independently via a wireless modem. They can have LCD or colour screens, and use specially adapted versions of PC applications such as Microsoft® Windows®, Outlook® Express and Internet Explorer.

Keeping it small

In order to keep PDAs small and lightweight, software manufacturers have devised versions of their programs that can run without needing a lot of power, and can be displayed on a small screen. To browse the World Wide Web, PDAs use a special kind of browser, called a microbrowser, which can show a Web page on a much smaller screen than an ordinary PC. Instead of a standard browser toolbar, for example, which would need a lot of screen space, you navigate back and forwards using tiny buttons on the PDA casing.

This PDA is resting on a "cradle" that connects it to a desktop computer.

Wireless connections

A number of telecommunications companies are working together to develop wireless connections between computers and other devices, using radio waves. This technology is called Bluetooth™, and is being incorporated in desktop and laptop computers, PDAs and mobile phones, making it easy to communicate between devices wherever you are.

What is more, different devices will be able to connect to each other automatically. For example, when you update somebody's contact details on your PDA, the new details can automatically be transferred to your mobile phone, your laptop and your desktop computer at home or at work.

Mobile phones

Mobile phones are even more convenient to carry around than PDAs, and they can incorporate a modem to connect to the Internet. They are also much less expensive than a PDA or a PC. However, traditional mobiles only have a tiny screen, and are not powerful enough to download lots of complicated data.

Mobile phones can be used to send SMS (Short Messaging System) text messages of up to 160 characters (the equivalent of four lines in this paragraph). Numbers on the keypad are used to type letters of the alphabet. Some phones use a system called "predictive text input" to guess the ending of a word when you start to type it, which can make typing faster and easier.

This phone can check e-mail and news services.

SMS can also be used for services such as news, sports results, financial updates and weather reports. Today far more text messages are sent via mobile phones than voice calls, and since about twice as many people own mobile phones as own PCs, there could be huge demand for Internet services on mobiles when they become available and affordable.

Early Internet phones

The first phones in Europe to connect to the Internet and download material used WAP (Wireless Application Protocol) format. WAP is a computer language used to present information very simply, usually as plain text, so that it can easily be downloaded and displayed on a very small screen.

WAP sites were designed to be like simplified Web sites for downloading to WAP-enabled phones. They made it possible to keep up with the latest news, manage a bank account, check cinema listings and book tickets, buy goods and even plan holidays. WAP phones could also send and receive e-mail, but in general WAP services were limited by WAP phones' small LCD screens.

A WAP phone

i-mode

The i-mode system in Japan has proved more popular than WAP, and gives a good idea of how Internet-connected phones may develop. i-mode phones have full colour screens and access to a range of services, from news and city guides to games and karaoke.

i-mode phones incorporate GPS (Global Positioning System), a technology which uses satellite to pinpoint exactly where you are anywhere in the world, within 20 metres. This can be used to obtain precise information for your exact position, such as local maps, traffic reports for your immediate area or route, or details of restaurants in the neighbourhood. You can even use your phone to ask for directions when you can't find your way back to your hotel!

A weather update

i-mode directions

"3G" phones

Many people have been looking forward to the introduction of "third-generation" or "3G" mobile phones in early 2002. (The original mobile phones of the 1980s, which communicated via analogue signals, are considered "first-generation"; the more compact and secure digital models of the 1990s, "second-generation".)

"Third-generation" phones make use of a technology called GPRS (General Packet Radio Service) to send large amounts of information at high speed in "packets" (see page 9). This makes it possible to incorporate colour and interactive features, including video phone and Internet access. To begin with, GPRS will operate at 384K, almost eight times as fast as a 56K modem, and will be "always-connected" for instant access to the Internet at any time. Some handsets will look similar to conventional mobile phones, others will have much larger screens and reduced keypads to make it easier to view Web pages.

Fourth-generation?

3G phones will represent a huge evolution, but technology experts are already looking ahead to super-fast 4G connections, perhaps as early as 2006. Who knows what kind of services we will expect to find on our mobile phones by then?

Mobile Internet Web sites

Find direct links to all these sites at **www.usborne-quicklinks.com**

Some of the most popular PDAs are made by **Palm**. See how they make Internet access possible on a small scale on their Web site.

Find out more about **Bluetooth** technology on the Bluetooth Web site.

NTT DoCoMo is the company that devised i-mode. It is also closely involved in developing 4G phones. The phone manufacturer **Nokia** has a good introduction to 3G and what it means.

Problems and solutions

Whether you are using your own computer at home, or you are part of a large business network, you will occasionally have problems connecting to or using the Internet. This section looks at some common problems, and what you can do about them.

What if I can't connect at all?

Sometimes your modem can have difficulty connecting to the Internet. This often happens when a lot of people are trying to go online at the same time and your ISP is busy. Your Dial-up Connection window may say "Unable to establish a connection".

If this happens, your Internet connection software may try again automatically, or you may have to click on the _Connect_ button to try again. Try once or twice more, and if this doesn't work, try again later. Ask your ISP when its busiest periods are, and try to avoid them. If you often have difficulty connecting, you may want to change your ISP.

Incorrect password If you have to type in a password, make sure that you type it correctly. Sometimes the system which accepts your password is "case sensitive", meaning that you have to use capital letters and small letters in the same places each time.

Authentication failed You may get an error message saying that your "authentication" has failed. When you try to connect, your modem sends a signal to your ISP's server. This signal, known as a handshake, tells the server who you are and confirms that you have permission to use it to connect to the Internet.

If your authentication has failed, it means your handshake has not been recognized. There may be a problem with your ISP's server, or you may not have set up your connection software properly. Call your ISP's helpline and ask for advice.

What if I can't pick up my e-mail?

If you are expecting e-mail and none has arrived, there could be several possible explanations.

Mail server fault There could be a problem with your ISP's e-mail server. If you still have access to the Web, you may be able to check this online: go to your ISP's home page, and look for a link to "Member services" or "Service announcements". If your ISP hasn't reported any faults, the problem may be with the sender's ISP. Usually ISPs are able to correct faults within a day or so.

Wrong address The person who is trying to contact you may simply have got your address wrong. Remember, it is important to get e-mail addresses exactly right, or a message will not be delivered. You could try sending them an e-mail so that they can check the address.

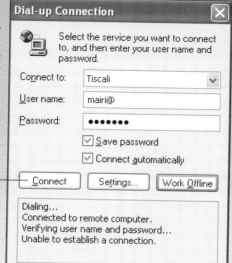

A Dial-up Connection window will tell you if you have a problem connecting to the Internet.

Click on this button to try to connect again.

Dial-up Connection

Select the service you want to connect to, and then enter your user name and password.

Connect to: Tiscali

User name: mairi@

Password: •••••••

☑ Save password
☑ Connect automatically

[Connect] [Settings...] [Work Offline]

Dialing...
Connected to remote computer.
Verifying user name and password...
Unable to establish a connection.

What if I get a virus via e-mail?

If you suspect that an e-mail contains a virus, delete it immediately without opening it. Make sure that you also delete it from your Deleted Items folder. If you get a virus warning via e-mail and you are not sure whether it is a hoax or not (see page 28), you could look for hoaxes of that name on a virus information Web site such as the F-Secure site, **www.f-secure.com/virus-info/hoax**.

If you do get a real virus via e-mail, contact your ISP as soon as possible and ask their advice.

Problems on the World Wide Web

Web connections are becoming better and more reliable all the time, but problems can still occur. The most common problems are: missing Web pages, pages with faults and Internet congestion (when a lot of people are using the Internet at once).

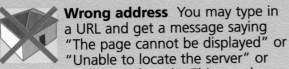

Wrong address You may type in a URL and get a message saying "The page cannot be displayed" or "Unable to locate the server" or "HTTP 404 – File not found". This may be a temporary connection problem. Try clicking on the *Refresh* button first of all. If this does not work, it could be because you typed the URL incorrectly – try typing again, and take care with endings such as .com or .org.

If you typed in a fairly long address such as **www.usborne.com/net_help/net_help.asp**, you could try "drilling down". This means taking away a part of the address after a slash (/) to try to get to another page on the same Web site. From there, you may be able to navigate to the page you were looking for.

Page unavailable If you still have no luck, the page may be unavailable because of problems with its host server, and you may be able to connect to it another time.

Page removed The page may have been taken off the Web altogether. Some sites put up messages when pages are removed, but not all do, and you may have to find what you are looking for on another site.

Change of address Sometimes Web sites change their URLs. Usually when this happens, you will find a message on the site of the original URL, giving you the new one. If the site was one of your Favorites (see page 42), you should change its URL using the *Organize Favorites...* command. Sometimes you will be redirected to the new site automatically, or you may have to click on the new URL to go to the new site.

Errors on the page The page may only partly download, and you may see a message saying that there are errors. Try clicking on the *Refresh* button.

Too slow

If Web pages take a long time to download, it can be very frustrating – and expensive, if you are paying for your time online.

Server problems There may be a temporary problem with the Web site's host server. Try clicking on the *Refresh* button first of all. The problem may also be caused by Internet congestion in general. Try connecting to the site later, when the Internet is likely to be less busy.

Slow browser, computer or modem If you generally find that Web pages take a long time to download, it may be that you have an old version of your browser. See if a more up-to-date version is available on the manufacturer's Web site. Or your computer may not be very powerful or you may not have a high-speed modem. You might want to consider replacing one or the other.

Safety Net

With millions of people using the Internet, there are bound to be those who misuse it. However, there are lots of precautions you can take that will ensure the Internet is a safe place to surf.

E-mail

Don't give your e-mail address out to strangers. You wouldn't give your home address out to a complete stranger, so why should your e-mail address be any different?

Be careful who you give your e-mail address to. Companies often ask you to fill out a form with your e-mail address on when you buy their products or download software from a Web site. Make sure that you can easily find their contact details on the site. Look for a box to tick, saying that you don't want to receive any advertising from the company, otherwise you may end up receiving annoying spam (see page 28).

Personal details

Many Web sites, especially shopping sites, ask you to fill in forms giving information including your name, address, e-mail address and telephone number, so that they can contact you to tell you about special offers. You should only ever give your details to well-known and well-established companies.

Most reliable Internet companies take good care of your details – check to see whether the site has a "privacy policy" which tells you that any personal details you give will not be misused or passed on to anyone else.

Meeting up

Someone you chat to online may suggest meeting up in real life. This is generally a bad idea. Remember that it is easy for people online to pretend to be somebody they aren't. If you can't see someone or hear their voice, you have no idea whether they are male or female, eight years old or 80. To avoid disappointments, or even danger, it's best to keep online friendships strictly online.

Viruses

Your computer can catch a virus if you copy files from an infected computer, or open an infected e-mail attachment. Viruses can spread rapidly over the Internet. The "I Love You" virus, for example, was released in May 2000 and had infected millions of computers around the world within 24 hours. It is now estimated to have caused up to $15 billion worth of damage.

Make sure that you have anti-virus software installed on your computer, and keep it up to date. For more about viruses, see page 16.

Hackers

Hackers are people who access computer systems without permission. They can link up their own computers to networks, and open private files. By reading or changing the information in these files, they may be able to steal money or goods.

If your computer is on a network, or an "always-on" broadband Internet connection, remember that other people may be able to access your files. Make sure you have some form of protection, known as a firewall.

If you are using a computer and a dial-up modem at home, it is very unlikely that people will try to access your files.

⚠ Internet potatoes

Some Internet facilities, such as games and chat, can become very addictive. If you are paying for time you spend online, this can prove very expensive. In addition, using a computer for any purpose for long periods of time can damage your health. It's essential to take a ten-minute break every hour that you use a computer, to rest your eyes and your body.

There's more to life than surfing the Internet. So make sure you don't become an Internet potato and end up at the receiving end of a common Internet insult... GAL, which means Get A Life!

Offensive material

People are free to publish whatever they like on the Internet. So, as well as interesting and worthwhile things, there's also unpleasant, unsuitable and dangerous information out there. Both Microsoft® Internet Explorer and Netscape® can be adjusted to block access to certain sites or reject certain kinds of material.

The Internet Options window in Internet Explorer

*To change the settings, click on **View – Internet Options** in the menu bar, then select **Content**.*

*Netscape has a similar feature under **Help – Netwatch**.*

You can also buy programs, called filters, that check and restrict the information you download from the Internet. You can change what these programs restrict to suit your own needs.

A filter program called Cyber Patrol®

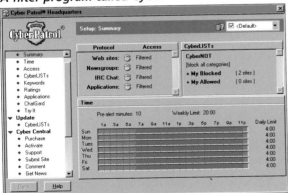

If you are in a chat room and somebody says something which makes you feel uncomfortable, don't respond. If they persist, inform the monitor of the chat room, or the online service providing the chat room.

Buying online

If you decide to buy anything over the Internet, make sure that the site you are buying from is secure before you give your financial details. A secure Web site will encrypt your details (translate them into code) so that they can't be used by anyone else. Both Microsoft Internet Explorer and Netscape show a closed padlock in the browser window when a site is secure.

Many people are concerned about Internet fraud, but although it is possible to commit a crime online, it is no easier than it is in the real world, and criminals are often easier to trace. For more information about safe shopping online, see page 67.

If a site is secure, Internet Explorer shows this padlock at the bottom of the browser window.

Internet protection

Find direct links to all these sites at **www.usborne-quicklinks.com**

If you often receive unwanted e-mail, you might try spam filtering software. One recommended spam filter is available as trialware from the **Spamkiller** Web site.

If you want to find information about a virus, try the **F-secure virus descriptions** page. The F-secure Web site also has the comprehensive list of **hoax warnings** mentioned on page 115.

If you are looking for anti-virus software, try the **Symantec™** Web site, featuring Norton™ AntiVirus, or the **McAfee®** Web site for McAfee VirusScan (for PCs) or Dr. Solomon's Virex (for Macintosh computers).

For filter programs, you could visit the Web sites of **Net Nanny®** and **Cyber Patrol®**.

Glossary

Here's a list of some of the Internet words you may come across, either in this book or elsewhere, with their meanings. The meanings given in this list are specific to the Internet. Some of the words have different meanings in other contexts.

Any word which appears in *italic* type is defined elsewhere in the glossary.

access provider see *Internet Access Provider*.

ActiveX® A Microsoft® product for including *multimedia* effects on *Web pages*.

address book A part of your *e-mail* program for storing other people's *e-mail* addresses.

address box The box in your *browser* window where you type a *URL*, or where a *URL* is displayed.

ADSL see *DSL*.

AIM (AOL Instant Messenger) see *Instant messaging*.

alphaware Very early trial versions of software.

animation A moving image made by showing a series of pictures in quick succession.

anti-virus software Software which protects your computer from *viruses*.

applet A small program produced with the programming language *Java*, which can be placed on a *Web page*.

application A program which enables your computer to create documents or perform tasks.

archive 1. The place on an *Internet host* where files are stored. 2. A *file* which contains one or more *compressed files*.

attachment A *file*, such as a text or picture file or *animation*, sent with an *e-mail*.

back-up A copy of a computer program or document.

backbone An important link between large *servers* on the *Internet*, which carries a lot of information at high speeds.

bandwidth A measurement of the amount of *data* that can flow through a link between computers. It is usually measured in *bits* per second (*bps*).

banner A piece of advertising across the top of a *Web page*.

BCC (blind carbon copy) A copy of an *e-mail* in which the person receiving the copy can't see who else the message has been sent to.

betaware Trial versions of software, more fully developed than *alphaware*.

bit The smallest unit of computer *data*.

body The main part of an *e-mail*.

bookmark Netscape® Navigator's way of storing a *URL* so that you can visit the *Web site* again quickly and easily.

Boolean query or **Boolean search** A way of refining a *search engine* search using special *operators*.

bounce When *e-mail* can't be delivered to its destination and is returned.

bps (bits per second) The basic measurement of how fast *data* is transferred.

broadband High-speed *data* transfer between computers.

browser A program used to find and display documents stored on the *Web*.

browsing Exploring the *Web*. See *surfing*.

bug A problem in a computer program which prevents it from working properly.

byte A unit of eight *bits*.

cable modem A very high-speed *modem* which uses the cable network (used for cable television) instead of telephone lines.

cache The part of a computer's memory where *Web pages* that have been *downloaded* are temporarily stored.

case-sensitive A system which recognizes the difference between capital letters and small letters.

CC (carbon copy) A copy of an *e-mail* to let someone know what you are saying to someone else.

chat Having a conversation with other *Internet* users by typing questions and answers.

chat room A *Web site* where a number of *Internet* users can *chat* at once.

client A computer which uses the services of a *host* or *server* computer.

clip art *Copyright*-free pictures which can be used to illustrate documents.

community A *Web site* which encourages visitors to share their views.

compression Making a smaller version of a *file*, so that it takes less space in a computer's memory, and less time to *download*.

cookie A *file* on your computer's hard disk which is used by *Web sites* to store information about you, such as when you last visited the site and which pages you *downloaded*.

copyright The legal obligation to obtain permission to reproduce text, music or images.

country code The part of a *URL* which shows where an organization is based.

crash A sudden failure in a computer system.

cyberspace The imaginary space that you travel around in when you use the *Internet*. The term is not often used these days.

data Information processed by a computer.

decompression Extracting a full-size *file* from a *compressed file*.

default 1. The automatic setting in an *application*, before you make any changes. 2. Often, the *HTML* name for a *home page*.

dial-up Using a *modem* and the telephone network to connect to the *Internet*.

digicam see *digital camera*.

digital Information recorded as a number code that can be read and processed by computers.

digital camera A camera that stores pictures as *digital data* that can be processed by a computer.

digital signature A short piece of *encrypted* text at the end of a document which can be used to identify the document sender.

directory A *search engine* which sorts *Web sites* into categories.

DNS (Domain Name Service) The system of giving organizations on the *Internet* names which are unique to them and can be recognized by other *Internet* users.

domain name The part of a *URL* which gives information about an organization, what kind of organization it is or where it is based.

down A computer or system which is not working.

download To copy a *Web page* or a program from a computer on the *Internet* to your own computer.

dpi (dots per inch) A measure of *resolution*.

drilling down Taking away parts of a *URL* in order to try and find other pages on the same *Web site*.

DSL (Digital Subscriber Line) A high-speed *Internet* connection via ordinary telephone lines.

e-mail (electronic mail) A way of sending messages via the *Internet* from one user to another.

embed To insert an image or a file in a *Web page* or other computer document.

emoticon see *smiley*.

encryption Translating information, such as financial information, into code to keep it secure.

expansion card A device, such as a sound card, that gives a computer extra features.

FAQ (Frequently Asked Questions) A *Web page* or a document used by *mailing lists* or *newsgroups* that lists the answers to questions often asked by new visitors or new members.

Favorites Internet Explorer's equivalent of *bookmarks* – a way of storing a *URL* so that you can visit the *Web site* again another time.

file Anything stored on a computer, such as a document, an image or a program.

file format The way a program stores information.

filter A program that checks *Web pages* or incoming *e-mail*, and blocks unwanted or undesirable content.

firewall A security system used to prevent unauthorized users from gaining access to a computer or a *network*, such as a company network.

flame An angry or rude *e-mail* or message sent to a *newsgroup*.

FlashTM A highly-developed form of *animation* used on *Web sites*.

follow-up A message sent to a *newsgroup* commenting on a previously *posted* message.

forum A discussion area on a *Web site*.

frame 1. A way of dividing up a Web page into separate areas to manage large amounts of information. 2. One of a series of images which make up an *animation*.

freeware Programs which can be *downloaded* and used free of charge.

FTP (File Transfer Protocol) A language used to transfer *files* over the *Internet*.

GIF (Graphics Interchange Format) An image *file format* often used for pictures on the *Web*.

guestbook A device that allows visitors to a *Web site* to leave their names and comments.

hacker Someone who gains unauthorized access to a computer or network, and may copy, change, destroy or steal information stored there.

header The part of an *e-mail* containing the sender's name, recipient's name, the date and message subject.

hit 1. A page found by a *search engine* which contains the *keywords* of the original *query*. 2. A visit to a *Web site*.

hit counter A device on a *Web page* which shows how often the page has been visited.

home page 1. The first page that *downloads* when you open your *browser*. 2. The first page that *downloads* when you visit a *Web site*, or the main page from which you can go to other pages.

host 1. A computer connected to the *Internet* which can give out information to other users. 2. An organization which runs a *Web site* for another organization or individual.

Hotmail® A popular free *e-mail* service, which can be accessed from any computer via the *Web*.

HTML (HyperText Mark-up Language) The computer code used to create *Web pages*.

HTML editor see *Web editor*.

HTTP (HyperText Transfer Protocol) The language computers use to transfer *Web pages* across the *Internet*.

hub A *Web site* containing news or other information to which people refer frequently.

hyperlink A piece of text or a picture that acts as a link from one *Web page* to another.

icon A symbol representing an *application*, an action or an object such as a picture or sound *file* on a *Web page*.

index 1. A *search engine* that lists millions of *Web sites*, and selects Web sites by matching *keywords*. 2. Often, the *HTML* name for a *home page*.

instant messaging A way of *chatting* to friends online in real time.

intellectual property see *copyright*.

interactive A *Web site*, or part of a *Web site*, which the user can respond to or change.

Internet The vast computer *network* made by linking computers together around the world.

Internet Access Provider or **Internet Service Provider** A company which offers users access to the *Internet*.

InterNIC (Internet Network Information Center) An organization in the US that gives out *domain names* and regulates their use.

intranet A *network* of computers within an organization, which can only be accessed by people in that organization.

IP (Internet Protocol) The language which allows computers to recognize each other over the *Internet*.

ISDN (Integrated Services Digital Network) A type of phone line that can transfer information between computers about twice as fast as a standard *56K modem*.

ISP see *Internet Service Provider*.

Java A programming language which can be read by all *platforms*, used to add *animations* and *interactive* features to *Web pages*.

JPEG (Joint Photographic Experts Group) An image *file format* often used for photographs on the *Web*.

K or **Kbps** Thousand *bits* per second, used as a measure of connection speed, as in "56K modem".

KB or **kilobyte** Approximately 1,000 *bytes*.

keyword 1. A word which describes a document's content. 2. A word used in a *search engine query*. 3. A word you type into the *address box* in AOL to go to another part of the service, such as Entertainment.

LAN (Local Area Network) A *network* of computers within an organization which is also connected to the *Internet*.

link see *hyperlink*.

log in or **log on** To connect to a computer, to a *network*, to an *online service* or to the *Internet*.

lurking Reading the messages in a *chat room* or a *newsgroup* without sending any yourself.

mailbox 1. The place where an *online service* or *ISP* stores new *e-mail* for you. 2. The place where *e-mail* is stored on your computer.

mailing list A discussion group where messages are sent to the group members via *e-mail*.

mail server A computer that handles *e-mail*.

MB or **megabyte** About one million *bytes*.

meta tag A *tag* that helps a *search engine* to classify a *Web page*.

MIDI (Musical Instrument Digital Interface) A way of transferring *data* between electronic musical instruments and computers.

MIME (Multi-purpose Internet Mail Extensions) The language used to transfer *e-mail attachments* via the *Internet*.

modem A device used to send and receive computer *data* across the telephone network.

MPEG (Moving Picture Experts Group) A *file format* used for audio and video clips on the *Web*.

MP3 A *file format* used for music clips which takes up very little computer memory without losing much sound quality.

multimedia Presenting information in various formats, which might include text, pictures, sound and video.

Net see *Internet*.

Netiquette The proper way to behave when using the *Internet*.

network A group of computers, *linked* so that they can share information and equipment.

newbie A new *Internet* user or a new member of a *newsgroup*.

newsgroup A place on the *Internet* where people with the same interests can *post* messages and see other people's responses.

offline Not connected to the *Internet*.

online Connected to the *Internet*.

online service A company that gives you access to its own private *network* as well as to the *Internet*.

operator A word or symbol which helps a *search engine* to make a search more specific.

packet A small piece of information sent over the *Internet*.

patch A short-term solution to a problem with a program, or protection against a *virus*.

pixel (picture element) A dot that is part of a picture. Everything that appears on a computer screen is made up of pixels.

platform The combination of a computer's *hardware* and the operating system it uses, such as a PC running Windows® or a Macintosh computer running the Mac operating system.

plug-in A program you can add to your *browser* to give it extra features, such as the ability to play sound or video clips.

POP (Point of Presence) A point of access to the *Internet*, usually a computer owned by an *ISP*.

POP 3 (Post Office Protocol) A system allowing you to collect your *e-mail* using any computer on the *Internet*.

portal A *Web site* that acts as a gateway to other sites.

post To send a message to a *newsgroup*.

proxy server A computer which connects a *network* such as a *LAN* to the *Internet*.

public domain Material which is not in *copyright* and can be used by anybody.

query An instruction to a *search engine* to find *Web sites* or information on the *Internet*.

RealAudio® A *file format* often used to play sound clips over the *Internet*.

register To give details about yourself on a *Web site* in order to receive information or software.

resolution The number of *pixels* that make up a picture. The higher the resolution, the clearer the picture.

scanner A device used to copy pictures or text from paper to a computer.

search engine A *Web site* which finds other *Web sites* or information in answer to a *query*.

secure server A computer that handles *encrypted* information, such as financial information, so that nobody else can read it.

Secure Sockets Layer or **SSL** An *encryption* system built into *servers* and *browsers* that uses "identity certificates" to recognize users.

serial port The part of a computer through which *data* can be transmitted to a *network*.

server A computer that carries out tasks for other computers on a *network*. Some servers hold information that other computers can *download*. Others act as *links* between individual computers or small *networks* and larger ones.

shareware Software which you use free of charge for a trial period.

smiley A picture made up of keyboard characters which looks like a face.

SMTP (Simple Mail Transport Protocol) The language used to send *e-mail* via the *Internet*.

source code The *HTML* code that makes up a particular *Web page*.

spam Junk *e-mail*.

streaming A format for playing sound or video clips directly as your computer receives the data over the *Internet*.

subscribe To sign up to a *mailing list*.

surfing Exploring the *Internet*.

table A way of arranging information or creating a structure for a *Web page*.

tag An *HTML* instruction that tells a *browser* how to display a certain part of a document.

TCP/IP (Transmission Control Protocol/ Internet Protocol) The language computers use to communicate with each other on the *Internet*.

thread A sequence of articles sent to a *newsgroup* forming a discussion on a subject.

timeout When a computer gives up trying to carry out a particular function, because it has taken too long.

trialware A basic version of a program which you use free of charge. You have to pay to use the full version.

unsubscribe To cancel a *subscription* to a *mailing list*.

upload To copy *files* from your computer to another computer via the *Internet*.

URL (Uniform Resource Locator) The unique address of a *Web page*.

Usenet The largest collection of *newsgroups* on the *Internet*.

username The name a person uses to connect to their *ISP*, which may also be the first part of their *e-mail* address.

virus A program designed to damage other programs, *files* or computers.

WAP or **Wireless Application Protocol** A simplified version of the *Web* which can be read using devices such as mobile phones.

WAV A sound *file format* developed by Microsoft®.

Web see *World Wide Web*

Webcam A camera that can take moving pictures which can then be attached to *e-mail* or inserted in *Web* documents.

Webcast A concert or other event which is broadcast on the *Web*.

Web editor A program you can use to create *Web pages*.

Webmaster A person who creates or maintains a *Web site*.

Web page A computer document written in *HTML* and *linked* to other documents by *hyperlinks*.

Webring A group of *linked Web sites*.

Web site A collection of *Web pages* created by an organization or an individual, having the same basic *URL* and usually stored on the same computer.

Web space The space *ISPs* make available for people to create their own *Web sites*.

WinZip® A popular *compression* program.

World Wide Web or **WWW** A vast store of information available on the *Internet*. The information is displayed on *Web pages* which are connected by *hyperlinks*.

WYSIWYG (What You See Is What You Get) A type of *Web editor* which shows you *Web page* content exactly as it will appear.

zipped file A *file compressed* using *WinZip*.

Useful addresses

You can find lots of useful information on the Internet to help you choose online services or ISPs. If you haven't set up your own Internet connection yet, you could use a computer in a library or ask to borrow a friend's. If you have particular questions in mind, look out for a FAQ (Frequently Asked Questions) page on the Web site to see if there is an answer there. There are some examples of questions on pages 12-13.

You'll find links to sites mentioned on this page at **www.usborne-quicklinks.com**

Online services

If you have access to the Internet, you can order connection software online. Otherwise, call the number for your country or area.

America Online (AOL)
in the UK: **www.aol.co.uk**
For connection software call 0800 376 5432

in the US: **www.aol.com**
For connection software call 1-800 827 6364

in Canada: **www.aol.ca**
For connection software call 1-888 382 6645

in Australia: **www.aol.com.au**
For connection software call 1800 265 265

CompuServe
in the UK: **www.compuserve.co.uk**
For connection software call 0870 600 0800

in the US: **www.compuserve.com**
For connection software call 1-800 292 3900

in Canada: **www.compuserve.ca**
For connection software call 1-888 353 8990

in Australia: **www.compuserve.com.au**
For connection software call 1300 555 520
In New Zealand call 0800 442 374

The Microsoft® Network (MSN®)
in the UK: **msn.co.uk**
For connection software call 08457 202000

in the US: **msn.com**
For connection software call 1-800 373 3676

Internet Service Providers

There are hundreds of ISPs in different countries around the world. Computer magazines regularly list and review ISPs and their services – before you decide on an ISP, it's worth reading some recent magazine reviews. In the UK, you'll find a list of ten recommended ISPs to suit different types of users on the **Internet Magazine** Web site.

You'll find users' opinions of different ISPs on the **epinions** Web site, which has sections for the US, Canada, the UK and Ireland. Do read a number of reviews to give you an all-round picture of a product or service.

Popular ISPs in the UK
Freeserve: **www.freeserve.com**
For connection software call 0990 500049

Tiscali: **www.tiscali.co.uk**
For connection software call 0800 542 1717

Virgin Net: **www.virgin.net**
For connection software call 0845 650 0000

Popular ISPs in the US
Earthlink: **www.earthlink.com**
For connection software call 1-800 395 8425

Juno: **www.juno.com**
For connection software call 1-800 879 5866

Prodigy: **www.prodigy.com**
For connection software call 1-800 776 3449

Canada
HomeFreeWeb: **www.homefreeweb.com**
Sign up online; for customer support call 905 948 0987

Sympatico: **pre.sympatico.ca**
For connection software call 1-800 773 2121

Australia
One.Net: **www.one.net.au**
For connection software call 1300 550 377

OzEmail: **www.ozemail.com.au**
For connection software call 132 884

New Zealand
Xtra: **www.xtra.co.nz**
For connection software call 0800 22 55 98

Index

@ (at), 18
3G phones, 113
acronym, 33
address book, 19, 26
alphaware, 47
animation, 44-45, 82, 83
anti-virus software, 16, 116, 117
AOL (America Online), 14-15, 18, 20, 34, 78, 123
applets, 45
attachments, 30-31
authentication, 114

back button, 41
backbone connection, 9
backgrounds, 90-91
betaware, 47
Bluetooth, 112
bookmarks, 42, 99
bps (bits per second), 11
broadband see High-speed connections
browser, 13, 17, 18, 34, 38-47, 67, 77, 78, 102, 112, 115
bulletin boards, 55

chat, 4, 6, 14, 78-79, 116
chat rooms, 79, 117
check boxes, 100
client software, 74
client, 8
clip art, 88, 96
colour, 87, 90-91
communities, 54-55
compression, 31, 46, 47, 95
CompuServe, 14-15, 20, 123
console (games), 11, 75
copyright, 43, 65, 82
copyright-free, 82
CPU, 10
crediting pictures, 88-89, 93

Dial-up Connection window, 17, 20, 21, 114
digest, 33
digital camera, 94
directories, 48-49, 54
display, see monitor
domain name, 18-19, 104, 105
dotcom companies, 3

downloading, 22, 40, 44, 46-47, 53, 64
downloading time, 103
dpi (dots per inch), 94
Dreamweaver, 81
drilling down, 115
DSL, 11, 110

e-card, 19
e-mail, 3, 4, 12, 18-31, 32, 37, 55, 67, 68, 101, 110, 114, 116
  deleting, 22, 28
  editing, 25
  forwarding, 23
  personalizing, 26
  printing, 22
  replying, 23
  storing in folders, 29
e-mail link, 98
e-mail signatures, 26
emoticon, see smiley
encryption, 67, 117
End User License Agreement, 46
error message, 41
exe (executable file), 30, 31

FAQ (Frequently Asked Questions), 37
Favorites, 42, 82, 115
Favorites button, 42
fibre optic cable, 9
file format, 95
filtering, 5, 28, 34, 51, 77, 98, 117
firewall, 116
flaming, 24, 34
Flash animation, 44, 45
Folders list, 22, 35, 84, 92
fonts, 87
formatting text, 84, 86-87
forms, 100-101, 105
form handler, 101
forums see bulletin boards
Forward button, 41
free Internet access, 13
freeware, 47
Form Field Properties, 101
FrontPage components, 100, 105
FrontPage Extextensions, 98, 100, 105

FrontPage, 3, 80-109
FTP (File Transfer Protocol), 105, 107, 109

gamepad, 74
games, 45, 46, 74-75, 116
GIF, 95, 96
Google, 50, 74
graphics card, 10

hackers, 116
HailStorm, 111
hard disk, 10
header, 22
helpline, 12, 114
high-speed connections, 3, 74, 80, 110, 116
History button, 42
hit counters, 98, 105
hits, 50, 51
hoax virus warnings, 28, 115
Home button, 41, 55
home page, 17, 39, 40, 84
  changing, 55
hosting, 104-105, 107
Hotmail, 18, 77
hotspots, 96
HTML, 81, 99
hubs, 54-55
hyperlinks, 39, 40, 48, 50, 83, 92-93, 96-97, 98, 99, 103, 106

icons, 16, 20, 22, 31, 36, 95, 96
i-mode, 113
Inbox, 22, 26, 28, 31
indexes, 48, 49, 50-51, 54
intellectual property see copyright
interactive Web sites, 45, 113
Internet connection software, 10, 12-13, 16
Internet Explorer, 5, 38, 42, 45, 47, 55, 112
ISDN, 11
ISP (Internet Service Provider), 12-13, 20, 22, 34, 35, 38, 39, 40, 54, 76, 82, 104, 105, 107, 114, 123

Java, 45

Acknowledgements

Every effort has been made to trace the copyright holders of the material in this book. If any rights have been omitted, the publishers offer their sincere apologies and will rectify this in any subsequent editions following notification.

Usborne Publishing has made every effort to ensure that material on the Web sites listed in this book is suitable for its intended purpose. However, we do not accept responsibility, and are not responsible, for any Web site other than our own. Nor will we be liable for any exposure to harmful, offensive, or inaccurate material which may appear on the Web. We recommend that children are supervised when using the Internet.

Usborne cannot guarantee that Web sites listed in this book are permanent, or that the addresses given will remain accurate, or that the information on those sites will remain as described.

Usborne Publishing will have no liability for any damage or loss caused by viruses that may be downloaded as a result of browsing the sites we recommend.
Screen shots used with permission from Microsoft Corporation.

Microsoft®, Microsoft® Windows®, Microsoft® Windows® 95, Microsoft® Windows® XP, Microsoft® Outlook®, Microsoft® Outlook® Express, Microsoft® Internet Explorer and Microsoft® FrontPage® are either registered trademarks or trademarks of Microsoft Corporation in the US and other countries.

Cover and p3:   c3: Virgin Records Ltd., used with permission.
Chateau de Versailles: used with permission.
CNN Interactive: used with permission.
Dexter's Laboratory™ and © Cartoon Network 2001. An AOL Time Warner Company. All rights reserved.
Fantasy Football: used with permission of CNN-Sports Illustrated Interactive.
The Hunger Site.com: used with permission.
Le Monde Interactif: used with permission.
Los Angeles city guide: © Time Out Group.
Moviefone: © 2001 America Online, Inc. Used with permission.
NME.com: used with permission.
Nokia: reproduced with permission of Nokia corporation. © Nokia Corporation 2001.
Sportal: © Sportal 2001
US Navy: used with permission.

Vogue: © Vogue.com UK, CondéNet UK Ltd. 2001. All rights reserved.

p6-7   Corbis Images: used with permission.
EyeWitness - History through the eyes of those who lived it: used with permission of Ibis Communications, Inc.
FCBayern: www.fcbayern.de, October 2001. Used with permission.
iht.com: used with permission.
Maporama: used with permission of Maporama SA
This is London: © www.thisislondon.co.uk
ViewSydney webcam: Sydney Harbour Foreshore Authority (photographer: Kim Hatton). Used with permission.
Virgilio: used with permission.
World Travel Guide: from worldtravelguide.net Used with permission.
With thanks to Amazon.com, Amy Miller Gray, the Guggenheim museum in Bilbao and U2.com.

p10-11   Gateway Profile 3 system computer: used with permission.
Modem used with thanks to 3Com, Inc.

p12-13   ClaraNet: used with permission of ClaraNet Ltd.
EresMas logo: used with permission.

With thanks to Club Internet, Earthlink and Tiscali.

p14-15 America Online: © 2001 America Online, Inc. Used with permission.
CompuServe: © 2001 CompuServe Interactive Services, Inc. Used with permission.
The Microsoft Network: used with permission.

p17 With thanks to Tiscali.

p18-19 E-card images: Digital Vision. Animation by Claudia Baggiani © 1994-2001 Yahoo! Inc. All rights reserved.

p30 Felix is a registered trade mark. Used under agreement with the trade mark owners.

p32 Basketball, saxophone, flowers, dolphin, motorcyclist: Digital Vision. Yahoo! Groups © 1994-2001 Yahoo! Inc. All rights reserved.

p34 Elvis: Pictorial Press Ltd. Used with permission.

p38 Eviaggi.com: used with permission.
FCBayern: www.fcbayern.de, October 2001. Used with permission. Home page of the Musée National d'Art Moderne at the Pompidou Centre, Paris: used with permission. With thanks to Barnes and Noble, El Mundo and Tiscali.

p40-41 bbc.co.uk: used with permission.
With thanks to NASA and the Smithsonian Institution.

p43 Portrait of Pierre Quthe, François Clouet (c.1522-1572), photo © RMN/J.G. Berizzi.
Bouquet of Flowers in an Arch, Ambrosius Bosschaert (1573-1621), photo © RMN/C. Jean
Self-portrait, Albrecht Dürer (1471-1528), photo © RMN/Arnaudet
The Tree of Crows, Caspar David Friedrich (1774-1840), photo © RMN/Arnaudet.

p44-45 MyCitySites – London: Less Rain; Barcelona: Vasava Artworks, SL. Used with permission.
With thanks to National Geographic.

p48-49 Yahoo! © 1994-2001 Yahoo! Inc. All rights reserved.
Volcano pictures: Boris Behncke, University of Catania. Used with permission.
Sagrada Familia: used with permission.

p50-51 AltaVista: © 2001 AltaVista Company. All rights reserved.
Google: Google Inc., used with permission.
Virtourist.com: used with permission.

p52-53 Ask Jeeves: reproduced with permission of Ask Jeeves, Inc.
Copernic: used with permission.
Mapquest (map of Georgia in screenshot): © 2001 America Online, Inc. Used with permission.
Images of Georgia: with thanks to the Parliament of the Republic of Georgia.
With thanks to Expedia and ixquick.

p54-55 news.bbc.co.uk: used with permission.
Benetton F1 and Sportal: © Sportal 2001
Guardian Unlimited: used with permission.
Virgin.net: used with permission.
With thanks to CNet.

p56-57 Background: Digital Vision. bbc.co.uk/reallywild: used with permission.
Discovery Channel: used with permission.
HowStuffWorks:© 2001, HowStuffWorks, Inc.
EyeWitness - History through the eyes of those who lived it: used with permission of Ibis Communications, Inc.
Naturalia: used with permission of EdV SRL (Gruppo Armando Testa SpA).

PBS/NOVA: photography, Canadian Scientific Submersible Facility. Used with permission.
Quid: used with permission.
With thanks to the Encyclopaedia Britannica, the History Channel, National Geographic and SprocketWorks.

p58-59 AFP: used with permission.
Babelfish: © 2001 AltaVista Company. All rights reserved.
news.bbc.co.uk: used with permission.
CNN Interactive: used with permission.
Gazeta.ru Ltd.: used with permission.
Guardian Unlimited: used with permission.
iht.com: used with permission.
Le Monde: used with permission.
With thanks to The Times.

p60-61 MapQuest and Moviefone: © 2001 America Online, Inc. Used with permission.
TimeOut: © Time Out Group.
With thanks to British Airways, Die Bahn and Streetmap.co.uk.

p62-63 British Museum: used with permission.
Château de Versailles: © Béatrice Saule. Used with permission.
Metropolitan Museum of Art: Lotiform Cup, Purchase, Edward S. Harkness Gift, 1926 (26.7.971). Photography by Schecter Lee © 1986 The Metropolitan Museum of Art, www.metmuseum.org © 2001 The Metorpolitan Museum of Art.
Museum of Modern Art, New York: used with permission.
National Gallery, London: used with permission.
Rijksmuseum: page design – Eden Design & Communication. © 2001 Rijksmuseum, Amsterdam.
With thanks to the American Museum of Natural History, the Guggenheim Museum in Bilbao, the Muséum national d'histoire naturelle and the Musée d'Orsay in Paris.

p64-65 Harmony Central: used with permission of HarmonyCentral.com, Inc.

NME.com: used with permission.
Nomad II MP3 player: with thanks to
CreativeLabs, Inc.
With thanks to Artist Direct and
Sony Music Ltd.

p66-67   Background: Digital Vision.
bol.com: Books On Line Italia SpA,
used with permission.
Kelkoo: used with permission.
MVC: used with permission.
Shopsmart: used with permission.
With thanks to Amazon.

p68-69   Background: Digital Vision.
Eviaggi.com: used with permission.
Food.com: courtesy of Food.com.
Lastminute.com: used with
permission.
Travelocity: used with permission of
Travelocity.com
World Travel Guide: from worldtravel-
guide.net Used with permission.
With thanks to Azierta, Expedia
and Tesco.

p70-71 Background: Digital Vision.
Médecins sans Frontières: used
with permission.
The Motley Fool: used with
permission.
NetDoctor: used with permission.
Patagon: used with permission.
KidsHealth.org: © The Nemours
Foundation. All rights reserved.
With thanks to Save the Children
and TheStreet.com.

p72-73 Snowboarder: © TempSport/
Corbis
CNN/Sports Illustrated Interactive:
used with permission.
ifyouski.com: used with permission.
Sports.com: used with permission.
TeamTalk: used with permission.
With thanks to the Bundesliga,
FC Barcelona, Juventus and
Olympique de Marseille.

p74-75   MSN Alchemy: used with
permission of Microsoft Corporation.
XTreme Snowboard:
© 2001 Bonus.com, Inc.
Xbox: with thanks to Microsoft.

p76-77   Yahoo! © 1994-2001
Yahoo! Inc. All rights reserved.
Excite screen display: © 2001 Excite
UK Ltd.
Internet cafe: Cyberia, Paris
©Frederick Froument

p78-79 Yahoo! Messenger © 1994-
2001 Yahoo! Inc. All rights reserved.
AIM: © 2001 America Online, Inc.
Used with permission.
With thanks to Cyberkids.

p80-81   Benjamin Camara: used
with permission.
Dreamweaver: with thanks to
Macromedia, Inc.
Josep Fornell: used with permission.
With thanks to Craig Williams, the
Reinhardt and Thiboutot families.

p82-83   Snapshots and flowers:
Digital Vision.

p88-89   Clip art courtesy of Clip Art
Warehouse.
Photos: Ian Britton, www.freefoto.com
Used with permission.

p90-91   Photos: Ian Britton, as before.
Background: www.motzmotz.com/
backgrounds Used with permission.

p92-93   Background and photos:
www.motzmotz.com and Ian Britton
as before.

p94-95   Hewlett Packard Photosmart
C315 digital camera and Epson
flatbed scanner, used with permission.
Icons: Clip Art Warehouse, as before.
Photos: Ian Britton, as before,

except skier: Digital Vision.

p96-97   The Infamous Grouse Band
is in no way associated with The
Famous Grouse Brand. Band logo
used on Web site with permission.

p104-105   Hewlett Packard Netserver
LC 2000, used with permission.
Freeserve: used with permission.
Homestead: used with permission.
Juno and the Juno logo are
registered trademarks of Juno Online
Services, Inc. Used with permission.
KataWeb: used with permission of
KataWeb SpA.
Terra: used with permission of Terra
Networks SA.
Tiscali: used with permission of
Tiscali SpA.
T-online: used with permission.
Wanadoo: used with permission.
Angelfire logo: © 2001 Angelfire, a
Lycos Network site. All rights reserved.
Yahoo! Geocities logo © 1994-2001
Yahoo! Inc. All rights reserved.

p110-111   Cables: © Lawrence
Manning/Corbis
Citroën Auto PC: used with
permission of Automobiles Citroën
France.
Recipe Web site: www.cuisineaz.com,
used with permission.
Soccer match: Ben Radford/Allsport.
With thanks to Electrolux.

p112-113   Ericsson early PDA: used
with permission.
i-mode: used with permission.
NewsFlash phone, WAP phone and
3G phone: with thanks to Nokia
corporation. © Nokia Corporation
2001.
PDA: with thanks to Palm, Inc.

117 Cyber Patrol: © 1998-2001
SurfControl plc.

First published in 2002 by Usborne Publishing Ltd., 83-85 Saffron Hill, London EC1N 8RT, England. www.usborne.com
Copyright © 2002, 2000, 1998, 1997 Usborne Publishing Ltd. The name Usborne and the devices 🔔 ⊕ are Trade Marks
of Usborne Publishing Ltd. All rights reserved. No part of this publication may be reproduced, stored in a retrieval
system or transmitted in any form or by any means, electronic, mechanical, photocopying, recording or otherwise,
without the prior permission of the publisher. Printed and bound in Great Britain by the Bath Press.